INSPIRED

SIMON GUILLEBAUD

STORIES OF ADVENTURE,
RISK-TAKING &
GOD'S FAITHFULNESS

10 Publishing
a division of 10 ofthose.com

Copyright © 2025 by Simon Guillebaud

First published in Great Britain in 2025

British Library Cataloguing in Publication Data
A record for this book is available from the British Library

ISBN: 978-1-83728-034-6

Designed and typeset by Pete Barnsley (CreativeHoot.com)

Printed in Denmark

10Publishing, a division of 10ofthose.com
Unit C, Tomlinson Road, Leyland, PR25 2DY, England

info@10ofthose.com
www.10ofthose.com

1 3 5 7 10 8 6 4 2

CONTENTS

INTRODUCTION

BY SIMON GUILLEBAUD

I felt some unease as I rounded the last bend on my motorbike, seeing a shifty figure a few hundred yards up ahead waiting outside my gate.

It was Aloys.

I couldn't quite make out what he disguised in his hand, but I discovered later it was a grenade. He planned to blow me up, it would seem.

I knew things were serious because he had written me a letter a few days earlier saying he was going to cut out my eyes. I'd had some sleepless nights over the threat, and informed the head of police. I'd also gone to stay at someone else's place and was varying my routes around town so that Aloys wouldn't know where to lie in wait.

My guard waved at me as a greeting, but it was actually a pre-arranged sign not to come any closer.

'God, what on earth shall I do? If it has to be, I'm ready to die. Let's go…'

What you have in your hands right now is a compilation of vivid snapshots from the life stories of seven friends of mine, who have seen and done remarkable things. Each of them shared their life experiences on the *Inspired* podcast. As so many people were impacted by listening to them, we wanted to catch some of the inspirational tales in a book.

So get ready to be challenged, stirred and blown away by these modern-day accounts of how God can lay hold of ordinary people who take him at his word, and how he does extraordinary things through them.

———— ✦ ————

As the host of the podcast, here is some of my story, by means of introduction.

Over a quarter of a century ago, I moved to the most dangerous country in the world – Burundi. I didn't know this was the case until my dear mother sent me a newspaper cutting with Burundi at number one on the list of places not to go if you were wanting to remain alive. (Was she hoping to encourage me?!)

I arrived in the middle of a civil war which eventually came to an end after twelve long years. It was a conflict that didn't make many headlines, but it dragged on and on. Everyone's heard of Rwanda because of the 1994 genocide in which about 800,000 people were killed in just three months. Well, at one time Rwanda and Burundi were one country called Ruanda-Urundi until the two kingdoms split at their independence from Belgium in 1962 into Rwanda and Burundi. So these two nations had a similar ethnic make-up (and tensions) of 85% Hutus and 14% Tutsis, although very divergent post-independence histories. In Burundi, the genocide started at the end of 1993 and continued far too long, with several hundred thousand people dying – but it wasn't as extreme as Rwanda's, hence being less well-known.

My arrival date was 10 January 1999. I'd had most of my money stolen in Rwanda by a 'friend', so was down to $300 in the world. That wouldn't last long, but instead of being anxious about it, I was excited because I knew God would be faithful in providing whatever I needed. How could I be sure? Well, I'd seen his hand so clearly already leading me up to this point.

Backtracking a few months, I'd been in London when I'd received a piece of paper with a name and number scribbled on it. 'This man's looking for you and wants you to give him a call.' It was the penultimate day of my year doing some theological studies on the Cornhill Training Course, and I'd been praying for months, 'Here I am, Lord. I'll do anything for you; I'll go anywhere for you!'

Thus far there had been a resounding silence, and time was running out. 'Lord, come on! I'm serious. I'll do anything, go anywhere. I don't want security. I just want to be in your will. That's the safest place to be!' Everyone else on the course seemed to have something lined up, but I was still waiting.

Little did I realise when I rang that number, making an appointment to meet the mystery man the next day, that my life was about to change radically. It was now the last day of the course. We met in St Helen's Church, Bishopsgate. I was intrigued. He said, 'My name's Robert de Berry. I lead an organisation called Mid-Africa Ministry. I've been praying, and I believe God has sent me to you and he's calling you to go to Burundi to be involved in youth, in mission and in evangelism.'

My heart thumped in my chest. Was this some random nut job? Either he was or, alternatively, God had sent him. We talked further and then parted, with my agreeing to pray about it and get back to him in due course.

For full disclosure, I, unlike most people, was already acquainted with Burundi. My great-grandfather is buried there; my great-aunt translated the Bible into Kirundi, the national tongue; my grandparents were the first *bazungus* (white people) to get married in Burundi. In short, there was a lot of Guillebaud family history in that part of the world. A year earlier I had driven a truck with friends through twelve countries from Wales to Kenya and then jumped on a *matatu* (taxi-bus) through Uganda into Rwanda and Burundi to spend time with my Granny and Auntie – who were teaching rural pastors in the north of Rwanda – and explore my heritage there. It was a precious experience, but I left assuming I'd never return. My desire was to go to a nation and people group which had never heard about Jesus at all, whereas both Rwanda and Burundi had fast-growing churches.

The Monday after my course ended, I returned to my previous place of work in marketing. My former employer had created a short-term position for me. I sat in front of my desk and prayed, 'Lord, if that Robert isn't a nut job but was actually sent by you, and if you do truly want me to go to Burundi, well… It's a dangerous place. It'll mean leaving family, friends, security, career, everything. It'll be a dramatic change. So please, as I fast and pray today, give me a radical sign right now in front of the computer about Burundi to justify such an extreme life-changing decision.'

The ball was back in his court.

I didn't have to wait long. I took a phone call in which, out of the blue, the voice on the other end said, 'Do you know anyone who wants to work in Burundi?'

Boom! I was off!

A few weeks later, after a family holiday and a farewell party, I packed my bags and was ready to leave. Then came the bombshell. Robert rang me to say, 'Simon, I'm really sorry. There's been some miscommunication with the folks in Bujumbura. I thought they were requesting a youth evangelist, which is why I approached you. But it turns out they want you to be the bishop's secretary.'

What? I had no desire to fulfil that role. I'm not the most ecclesiastical of people, and that position didn't align with my passions, skills or calling. But it was too late. I'd had the farewell party and had to go! So I flew to Rwanda, initially to live with my Granny and Auntie. The former would teach me the basics of the language for four months before I headed south to Burundi.

I flew out in some confusion, now lined up for a job I didn't want, but ultimately trusting the Lord. My consistent prayer was along the lines of: 'Lord, have mercy on me! I don't want to be secretary for the bishop. Please let me work with Scripture Union as a non-denominational organisation with access to all the youth nationwide.'

Granny and Auntie Meg joined me in that prayer over those four months together. The internet was new back then and I set up an email address for the first time to ask a few dozen friends in England to pray the same prayer. Unknown to me, Scripture Union (SU) in Burundi had heard that a *muzungu* (foreigner) called Simon was coming in January, and they were praying God would direct him to them.

Can you see the threads coming together?

On the last night of my time in Rwanda, Granny prayed me off: 'God, we've had enough of Simon! He's surrendered to you, so just make it clear whether you want him to be secretary for the bishop or evangelist with Scripture Union.'

I said goodbye and headed to friends in the Rwandan capital, Kigali. I stopped off for just ten minutes at the SU guesthouse to greet Robert, who had just arrived from London. At that very same moment, the head of SU Burundi arrived on a three-day drive to Kenya. It was extraordinary timing. Here were three different men, from three different countries, in transit to two different countries, praying the same prayer, meeting in the same guesthouse in the capital city at the exact same time! Coincidence? No, rather a God-incident! The bishop too saw God's hand and released me to work with SU instead (which in retrospect was a very magnanimous but costly decision to him personally).

I love the nugget hidden in 2 Chronicles 16:9 which says, 'For the eyes of the LORD range throughout the earth to strengthen those whose hearts are fully committed to him.' That was my heart's desire – total surrender, full commitment, anywhere, anytime, bring it on!

And to God's glory, the outworking of that prayer more than twenty-five years later has been literally hundreds of thousands of lives coming to Jesus, through developing a wonderful expanding network of hardcore Burundian disciples being mobilised and equipped for the transformation of the nation. What a privilege!

There are too many stories to tell, but that first day in Burundi – remember, I had just $300 left – I found an internet café and sent out my first email ever from there (of what became just under 200,000 over the coming two decades). I wrote to my small group of prayer supporters, 'Folks, keep praying. I trust God to open up the way for me to work at SU. And I really need a computer!' That very morning, a friend woke up and prayed, 'Father, I sense you're telling me to give my computer to someone. Show me who.' He turned on his computer and got my request from central Africa for a computer!

I love God's promises in his word, and one I have claimed time and time again is: 'And my God will meet all your needs according to the riches of his glory in Christ Jesus' (Philippians 4:19). He would go on to do that repeatedly in the following years. Note that the promise is to meet our needs, not our wants.

Even that first weekend, the SU team wanted to show me that they were active, so they organised a weekend of evangelism up-country. Unfortunately, because of an international embargo and the ongoing civil war, the economic situation was dire. SU was bankrupt, had debts and staff hadn't been paid in two years. They had one pathetic excuse of a vehicle, which was a risk to drive through rebel-controlled territory. But we went for it! Sure enough, it sputtered to a halt in the hills and we broke down five times that day on the most dangerous roads in the world. I remember thinking as we were sitting ducks on the roadside, 'Am I going to die on my very first weekend here? That'd be a bit of a waste!'

We eventually crawled into town later that evening, having missed one of the two days of activities. I wrestled with God, 'Come on, Lord! Folks missed out on hearing the good news today because of our useless vehicle. Please, get us out of debt and with a vehicle that works by the end of the month!' For that prayer to be answered, we needed £15,000, which was a huge sum to me at that time. But sure enough, £15,000 came in by the end of the month, including a cheque for £5,000 made out 'for a vehicle', which the generous giver could not have been aware was a crying need.

I look back on those early days with amazement and gratitude. My amazement is because God did so many beautiful things through us. My gratitude is because we survived to tell the tale. I genuinely expected to die. Others did die. Once, after driving through the hills, I found out that forty people had been killed in four different ambushes. One time I was cruising along with a colleague, he said with a glint in his eye, 'Isn't it exciting, Simon? We are immortal until God calls us home!'

It was thrilling to be completely trusting God day-by-day, but there was a price to pay as well. This price involved seeing so much suffering; receiving death threats; grieving for others who were killed; contracting many varied tropical diseases; being betrayed and slandered; the breakdown of relationships; separation from family and friends back home…

…but now Burundi was my home. Indeed, in due time I became Burundian. Now I – together with my wife and three children – are five of maybe only a dozen white Burundians in the world. Lizzie agreed to marry me back in 2003. My proposal, made while slightly delirious with malaria, included the winsome invitation: 'Are you ready to be a young widow?' She counted the cost, agreed and became a wonderful partner in the work.

That same year, Great Lakes Outreach was set up as a vehicle to support not just Scripture Union but a burgeoning network of superb leaders working across many spheres of society for the transformation of the nation. Peace came in 2005 and lasted for a decade. During that time, Lizzie and I started a family, and the work exploded in growth and impact. Sadly, in 2015, there was renewed violence and Burundi to this day is one of the poorest and hungriest countries in the world.

A lot more detail on that journey is covered in my book *Dangerously Alive: African Adventures of Faith under Fire*. My spiritual logic and DNA involves asking the question: how far is too far when Jesus stretched his arms wide on the cross and went that far for us? I dream of being part of an army of servant-hearted, bold, risk-taking Jesus-followers who act justly, love mercy and walk humbly with their God in whatever context they find themselves. Hopefully you're one of them!

As we embark on this book together, let me whet your appetite at the start.

You will read of **Rachael Mutesi**, a fearless Ugandan woman who rose from the humblest of backgrounds to study at Oxford, and who has chosen to return to live in the slums of Kalerwe. She risks her life fighting for the rights of sexually abused girls, and is heroic in being a voice for the voiceless and marginalised.

Next is **Sarah**, who right now chooses to live in a nation in south-east Asia with ongoing conflict and violence. She has to be wise in how and when she shares her faith because the regime in place is antagonistic to the gospel – so much so that we can't even name this country.

Then there's **Duncan Dyason**. He had a criminal record by the age of thirteen before being dramatically converted. He ended up spending over three decades in Guatemala working among street children, where he has seen the situation transformed to such an extent that there are almost no more street children now in the whole country. My favourite story of his is of the hitman who came to kill him but first allowed him to preach the gospel, at which he melted and admitted he'd tried to shoot Dunc in the head a few days earlier but the bullet simply hadn't fired. So Dunc's still alive, and his contribution to Guatemala was recognised by Queen Elizabeth with the award of an MBE.

Alli Blair is one of my best friends and a total eccentric! We spent a couple of decades together in Burundi, and she took plenty of risks in the war years. In fact, I suspect we were the two most likely white people in the whole country to get killed because of our constant travels through rebel-held areas. But now, as you read this, picture her in a hammock in the jungles of northern Cambodia, with rats and pigs squeaking and squealing around her as she seeks to promote the translation of the Bible into Kavet to help that isolated people group come to Jesus.

David Campbell was expelled from his first boarding school, and then as a seventeen-year-old he disappeared mid-term from his next one. Most kids who run away from school at least stay in the same country rather than flying to another continent. But David cashed in his savings and flew to Jamaica to start a new life! Guns, knives and drugs were his new patch. His story could only have been woven by God's guidance and protection as he engaged with the toughest of Trench Town. His work was also recognised with the award of an MBE.

Dieudonne Nahimana's father was buried alive in a pit during the 1993 genocide in Burundi, so Dieudonne was left on the streets in the war with nothing. But having tasted the life of a street-connected child, he founded an organisation to rescue such children and give them a hope and a future. Forgiving his dad's killers, he returned to the spot where his father was murdered and spoke to one of his murderers, then preached reconciliation there. As if that wasn't enough, though that man has now died, Dieudonne is sponsoring the children of his father's murderer through school. How do you do that? Dieudonne actually stood as a presidential candidate in the 2020 elections and changed the whole tone of the debate, helping to keep violence and bloodshed at bay.

Marcia Suzuki's story is almost unbelievable in the true sense of the word. It encompasses ending up in the deepest jungle, working with a naked tribe, getting infanticide outlawed in Congress in Brazil and having to subsequently flee the country.

Wow!

So get ready to read about some modern-day miracles, to be challenged to imagine what might be possible in your life, and to be inspired to count the cost and be 'fully committed' to God. Remember: 'For the eyes of the LORD range throughout the earth to strengthen those whose hearts are fully committed to him' (2 Chronicles 16:9). May that be you, dear reader!

Enjoy, and be inspired!

1
RACHAEL MUTESI

UGANDA

Kampala, Uganda – 1990s

A pain in my foot woke me with a jolt. Something bit me. I sat up, just in time to see the silhouette of a rat scuttling away into the darkness. I rubbed my toes and lay back down on the thin mattress my mother had made with leftover cotton from the fields. She was sleeping next to me on the floor, along with my older sister.

Even though it was night, light came through the many holes in the walls of our mud-brick home, which doubled as the school storeroom. The air was warm, but I wrapped my t-shirt around my feet in case the rat decided to come back. A dog barked and I could hear drunk people laughing in a shack bar not far away. This was Kalerwe, my home, a slum built on a swamp in Kampala, Uganda.

Waking up in the morning, I felt tired from my interrupted sleep.

'Lakeeri, time to get up,' my mother called as she boiled water for tea over the charcoal stove. Hot black tea and half a sweet potato from the night before was breakfast before school started at 8 a.m. Maama had already collected the water we needed from the well that served the whole community.

My sister, Resty, and I were grateful to be in a position to go to primary school – as it was sponsored by World Vision, we could go for free. Maama had a certificate in nursery teaching, so she was offered a job as a nursery teacher, and we lived in the school compound.

As money was scarce, I was often hungry. So when World Vision announced they were having 'centre days' at the school on Saturdays where you would get a bowl of rice, I was keen.

At the centre days, my sister and I were taught songs like 'Shine Jesus Shine' for a Diocesan concert called 'Celebrate Jesus'. This concert was for children's ministries all across Kampala and took place in 1999, when I was nine years old. There was praise and worship, and different tents where you could hear Bible stories. I would have called myself a Christian as I went to church with my mother each Sunday, but it was not a living faith. At 'Celebrate Jesus' I felt I heard the gospel properly for the first time, and I wanted to become a Christian. All I can say is that I was radically changed from making that decision.

I went back home and told Maama, 'I've become a Christian.'

She smiled and said, 'Well done, my daughter.'

On Monday at school I also declared to my friends, 'I've become a Christian' and asked my teacher if I could be the religious prefect. I started reading Maama's Bible every chance I had, and my favourite game was to make a little pulpit for myself out of stones to preach what I learnt to my friends.

As the weeks went by, not only was my heart changed, but my body got stronger. I had been a weak, sickly and sad child, but my relationship with Jesus brought me deep joy.

My parents had divorced when I was a few months old and so I only saw Baaba, my father, about once a year. My sister and I would go and visit him and his other family in their village eighty kilometres away in Jinja. Baaba was from a well-to-do family and did not like to come to the slum.

When I graduated primary school top of my class, he was amazed. 'You have surprised me, Lakeeri,' he said.

'Why Baaba?' I asked, confused.

'Because I thought you would die.'

I believe I lived because God gave me hope, but I knew my father wasn't alone in his assumption that I would not make it to adulthood. Death was very present in my life. By the time I was twenty, half of my school friends had died from diseases like cholera. There were no toilets so people went wherever they felt like, and when it rained, the sewage flooded through the houses. Malaria was also a serious problem as the swamp we lived on was infested with mosquitoes.

I finished high school with the help of my Uncle David, who was a teacher. He got my sister and me scholarships into the top schools he worked in so we could take A Levels. I chose physics, economics and mathematics because, at that time, the government was starting to sponsor female students who did science subjects.

I worked hard and hoped I had done well enough for a government scholarship for university. When Maama called the school on results day, my heart sank as I realised my maths marks were not good enough for a scholarship.

'I can't help you, Lakeeri,' Maama said sadly. All her money was going to send my older sister to medical school; there was nothing left for me. And I could not ask my father for help as he had multiple wives and was already paying for my siblings' education. Besides, he had rejected my mother and I felt that personally, so was not confident to go to him.

'Why don't you look for work in a school,' she suggested. 'You are good with children, and you can save money for university.'

I had taught Sunday school from the age of eleven, so I knew how to teach children. It seemed like a good idea. I applied to work at a local school, but after the first month I was never paid. This happened in five schools in total. My employers took advantage of me because I was young and they knew I couldn't report them since I wasn't a qualified teacher.

I then got a job at a boarding school a thirty-minute walk from home. I was offered 80,000 shillings a month (about £20) to be the school matron. There were fifty children between the ages of three to twelve in the school. I slept in the dormitory with the younger kids and was like a mother to them, helping them get ready for school in the mornings.

At the end of the month, the head teacher invited me to his office. He was a man in his fifties and I was eighteen.

'Rachael, I see you have been helping the children with their maths homework. You are a good teacher and we want to keep you,' he said.

I was encouraged by what he was saying, but when he went to close the door behind me, I began to feel uncomfortable.

He smiled, but it didn't make me feel better.

'We want you to come and teach mathematics, and we're going to increase your salary from 80,000 to 150,000 shillings. But…' he said, with a glint in his eye, 'this is on condition that you will sleep with me. Every woman that has worked in the school has slept with me.'

I gasped, but he didn't seem to notice my horror. 'We can either do it here, or you can decide the place,' he said.

I started shaking my head. How could he think I would do this? I was a Christian, and that meant sexual purity. I would not sleep with a man until I got married.

'I cannot sir,' I said firmly.

'You need this job, don't you?' he snarled. 'Just look at this as what you have to do to get to university.'

'I am a believer, I will not,' I said. My voice was shaking.

His face screwed up in anger and he lunged at me, trying to rip my clothes off. I was very small compared to him, but I fought him with all my might. Internally I was praying, *'God help me!'*

We wrestled for a good ten minutes until suddenly someone starting knocking loudly on the office door. A woman's voice shouted, 'Master, master, please come out. I saw you walk in. We need you urgently.'

My attacker started to panic. He jumped off me and straightened his clothes, which gave me a chance to run to the door and escape.

I went back to the dormitory, saying a silent prayer of thanks to God for saving me, and packed everything I had. I left the school, never to return.

'Lord show me what to do to pay for university,' I prayed. Eventually an idea came to me. My aunt had taught me how to make samosas; I decided to try selling them. For three years every day, Maama and I woke up at 3 a.m. to make samosas. Then I took them to the market to sell before my classes started. This is how I paid for my studies.

By the grace of God I was able to finish at Makerere University with a Bachelors in Commerce, majoring in marketing. While I studied I joined a ministry that shared the gospel in schools around the country. Every weekend I would be out with a team at a different school. In 2012 I also started Kingdom Daughters, a ministry to empower vulnerable girls, helping with menstrual poverty and identity issues.

Norwich, England – 2013

While I was studying at university, I also volunteered with an evangelistic organisation on the weekends. A father and daughter from the UK came as part of a team to work with us. We all got on so well that they arranged for me to go to the UK after my degree to spend a year with Youth for Christ in Norwich. Two lay readers from my church, the priest, my family and other members of the congregation all travelled to the airport with me – it was such a big deal that I, a slum girl, was flying to the UK! When we arrived at the check-in area, my church family sang worship songs and then they prayed for me. Then one of the lay readers, who was like a grandmother figure to me, read out a verse in Deuteronomy. She said, 'Remember it is God who will bring you to the promised land. It is God who elevates the humble. God will carry you through and you don't have to be afraid.'

Her words gave me confidence, as I only had 1000 shillings (25p) in my pocket, and I had never left Uganda, let alone flown on a plane.

On my first flight to Doha, after my food plate was delivered to my seat, I tasted cheese for the first time! When we landed in Doha airport, I realised I was going to have to use the escalators to get to my next flight. I had never seen moving stairs before and was terrified. I spent a long time hovering at the bottom of the escalators, too scared to step on, until a kind American man took me by the arm and guided my shaking body onto the first step. I was very relieved. Finally arriving in England, in the summer, I was cold – and always stayed cold!

In November I was invited to a Healing of the Nations Conference, held in Derbyshire. It was there I met the parents of the apologist Amy Orr Ewing. Her father, Dr Hartmut Kopsch, is a pastor and a Bible teacher. At the end of conference I was asked to say the closing prayer.

Now there is a difference between a prayer from the west and a prayer from Africa. Our prayer is another sermon!

I started praying with all the passion and fire I had inside of me. It was about 10 p.m., and I prayed for forty minutes. My eyes were closed so I was not aware of the shocked faces of those who assumed I would pray for a few minutes! Dr Hartmut Kopsch came up to me afterwards and said, 'That's what they call a closing prayer.'

And then he added, 'The call of God upon your life is remarkable. God has called you to be a fearless evangelist.' He invited me to visit him and his wife. There they took me to Cheltenham to hear Amy speak at an event on Micah 6:8: 'What does the LORD require of you? To act justly and to love mercy and walk humbly with your God.'

As I sat in the audience, I thought, I've never seen a woman preach like this, with so much clarity and power. I wanted to be able to communicate like her. I wanted to be trained as a woman who is qualified to be on a platform.

I explained this to her parents, and they invited me to apply to study at OCCA – The Oxford Centre for

Christian Apologetics, an accredited branch of Oxford University. It's a place where people come to be equipped on the basics and fundamentals of Christian theology and to get an understanding of why we believe what we believe. When I went to the interview I didn't even know what apologetics meant, but I told them I wanted to be an evangelist, and somehow I got in!

Oxford, England – 2014

I loved the missions at OCCA, where we were able to go to universities and preach the gospel. I remember one mission to a university in Kent. For the first three days no one came to the Lord, and then on the last day about fifty-seven students came to faith.

When I came to the OCCA, I was focused on sharing the gospel, but as I told my stories, people were shocked at what I thought was normal – like girls being gang raped. I had grown up with so much sexual violence that I had become desensitised. Seeing the reactions of my friends, my heart opened to the injustices that I had been brought up with. When I returned to Kalerwe, I wanted to change the status quo.

The week I returned from the UK, I decided to start a community choir, inspired by the gospel choir that we ran in Norwich Youth for Christ. My choir was to be for the girls who didn't go to school. I would invite them and prepare them a meal, and then we would sing. At our first meeting, one of the girls asked, 'What do you do if you hate your father? How do you kill him?'

Of course, the other kids looked astonished. I talked to the girl and she revealed that her father was abusing her. He worked in the countryside between Monday to Friday, returning home every Saturday. Their family had a small house where about five of them lived, with a curtain separating the bed from the sitting room. She said, 'Every day I put on extra pants that he won't do it. But my mum doesn't come out to save me, and he does.'

I said to her, 'You know what, I will figure it out.' And I went to a pastor friend of mine, from an affluent church, and shared the girl's story. I saw the apathy in her eyes as she replied, 'Rachael, three-year-olds in the slum are being abused. This girl is eleven – she can handle it.' I realised she didn't want to get involved and thought it was a waste of time me getting involved. I disagreed.

The only alternative we had was to move that girl into a boarding school, and so that's what we tried to do. Boarding schools are the main way to get girls out of abusive situations. If they are pregnant, we take them to a pregnancy crisis centre where they can get more support than we could offer.

In 2018 we registered Ufahari Girls Ministries. Part of my mission changed to take care of neglected children, particularly those who have suffered from sex violence.

There is research that shows that girls not in school are three times more likely to be abused than those who are in school. So I started asking, 'Why are these girls out of school?' When covid happened, I realised parents were prostituting their children in exchange for food. Right now we have seventeen girls in our care. Each of those girls has the same story: 'My mother brought a man to sleep with me so that we could get a kilogramme of rice to survive,' or 'My grandmother sent me to my uncle to get food and he abused me.' We also have an eight-year-old girl who was sent to a bar to work so that her father could get free alcohol.

Remembering what Amy Orr Ewing said, I asked myself, 'What does the Lord require of us?' The Lord requires us to have mercy, and that means drawing these girls out of those communities and finding safe alternatives for them. At the moment that is putting them in boarding school.

The thing about African culture is that there is a lot of secrecy around sex violence. Recently I listened to the story of an eight-year-old called Rasheeda. She was sent to go and buy food, but was attacked by a herdsman and raped. She carried on home, but in the process spilled the maize flour. When she returned home bleeding, she was punished for spilling the food. After she told me the story, I asked, 'What can I do for you?' She said, 'I need to have that guy arrested'. And by the grace of God, we were able to do that.

The mother of another girl, called Hawa, told me, 'Oh, the only thing that happened is that my daughter was molested. No one can hear she was abused.' I planned a little retreat for the girls about two weeks ago, but Hawa's mother said, 'My daughter cannot go.' She refused because then everyone would see Hawa as dirty. Families will rather pretend sex violence didn't happen, because it seems the safe thing to do. And so then these girls are forced to be resilient, because no one is challenging the status quo.

———— ✈ ————

I've had countless threats of being poisoned, because we have been able to put perpetrators in prison, and they don't forgive us. So I'm very, very careful what I eat in the community. I don't allow people I don't know into my house – that's the rule I hate most, but it is just a way to protect myself.

There have been times when I've been attacked in the community. I remember one time when we had just succeeded in getting a guy arrested who had abused a five-year-old. His family was unhappy, and were hurling insults at me. When I was walking in an isolated part of our community, just rushing to get a lift, suddenly I was surrounded by these guys. They had knives and had come to attack me.

One of the men looked like he recognised me. He said, 'Are you Auntie Jessica's daughter?'

Jessica is my mum. I nodded.

'Her mum taught us, she loved us, she took care of us,' he said. He told the guys to back off, and then they walked away!

I was terrified and thankful at the same time. They could have killed me and no one would have realised.

Just a moment after that, I got into a taxi, and there were two male passengers in the vehicle. They locked the door and one guy said, 'You're so beautiful.' I don't normally hear people say that to me. He then pulled me onto his lap and tried to kiss me. I was screaming and trying to get free. Thankfully it was about 9 a.m. and we were in a busy area, so people realised what was happening and the guy released me.

I know that these are just things that have been set up to terrify me into stopping, but I will not stop.

Kampala, Uganda – 2020

One day I saw an advert for a six-month fashion and dressmaking course called Motiv. It would cost 50,000 shillings (approximately £10) a month, and would provide a new skill that I thought would be helpful for the girls. We had been given sewing machines and were making reusable sanitary towels, but I knew there was more we could do. I was able to enrol myself and five of our girls on the course. I wanted to show them there is no shame in upskilling projects, as many felt vocational skills were for those who had failed.

The six of us got on the back of three boda boda motorcycle taxis to weave our way through the busy Kampala traffic to where the course was held twenty minutes away. When we arrived at Motiv, I bumped into a friend, Konso. We had done a mentoring project together the year before called Project Soar. I noticed a guy, Calvin, taking photos as we worked, and it turned out Konso knew him. She introduced us and we chatted. He was a gentle, quiet guy. He said he had been working on a documentary about teenage mothers, but kept on being refused entry in places. Many African churches look down on people that have locks and tattoos and he had both. I said to him, 'I work with girls, I might be able to help you.'

We arranged to meet for a coffee a few days later to talk about working together. I had also written some poems that I wanted him to put images to.

Before we met again, I had to go to hospital with one of our girls who had become extremely suicidal. She had been raped, got pregnant, tried to terminate the pregnancy and caught an infection. Everything was going wrong. After being with her for seventy-two hours, I came back to help another girl who had lost a child and been abandoned by her family. Then another child that I know was raped.

After all that, I went for coffee with Calvin. He just listened as I talked through it all. We ended up speaking for three hours. He paid for my drink, and then paid for my boda boda home. 'Let me know when you get home safely,' he said.

I thought then that if he asked me out I would say yes, but I didn't think it was likely as he was five years younger than me.

However when we started to work together, we soon realised we were both interested in each other!

Calvin and I married in August 2022 and now run Ufahari Girls Ministry. We are supporting many girls. Our vision is to amplify the voices of those girls who are being abused. This conversation has been suppressed too long. It is upon us to tell their story so that society is awakened to the reality of what is happening, particularly in slum communities.

Last year eight of our girls graduated from school. One of them got an internship and then a job with the Uganda Broadcasting Corporation (UBC). She has invited me to come and speak there. When I was younger I dreamed of being a journalist. I went to the UBC to ask if I could volunteer, but I looked so scrawny and poor I wasn't even allowed past the entrance. Now I am welcomed in, all through one of the girls we helped!

The future

Our dream is to have a school. When a girl comes to Christ, it is as if God is the foundation and the building, while education is like the plastering on the house – it gives purpose, meaning and direction. We want to build a boarding school that can be like a family, and give a safe place to more children.

Our love for God should push us to express love for others. My favourite Scripture is when Jesus said, 'Whatever you did for one of the least of these brothers and sisters of mine, you did for me' (Matthew 25:40). The question to ask always is, who are the least among us?

The moments when I despair I pray, 'God I'm not sure if I can handle this.' He gives me his grace to live each day at a time, to help the next person in front of me. I think the thing that has grounded me has been hope in Christ. It is only Jesus who can bring healing and restoration.

2

SARAH

SOUTH-EAST ASIA

I haven't always loved Jesus. In fact I spent most of my time at boarding school – in England – trying to get out of chapel and ending up in detention as a result. If you would have told me that I would extravagantly love and radically obey Jesus with my life, I would have laughed in your face. I was spiritually hungry, just not for Jesus.

During my teenage years and into my early twenties, the echo chamber within me reverberated with one short penetrating lyric from Michael Jackson's song 'Heal the World': 'Stop existing and start living'. I pursued my spirituality through new age practices and the pursuit of the next high or the next location: psychics, drink, drugs and travelling! This heady cocktail made me feel alive, but there was always the need to return to normal life or to face the comedown.

I was part of that generation that hit the road to explore the world and all it offered. But once uni and gap years ended, was life really just about getting a job, getting married, having kids and living for the day when you could take drugs with them?

After I graduated from university, I hit the road for one final summer of freedom. While staying in Prague, a love of architecture – and nothing more – led me to St Vitus Cathedral. I woke early in an attempt to avoid the mass of people on my visit, but I was so early that the cathedral doors were firmly shut. I sat on a bench outside waiting. Two Asians strode purposefully towards me and, smiling with great enthusiasm, asked me at point-blank range, 'Do you believe in God?' Sitting in such close proximity to what I understood at that time to be his residence, I fidgeted awkwardly and gave a non-answer. Who knows what they thought, and I certainly didn't sit around long enough to find out, but the question bounced around irritating me within.

My travels next took me to France and the home of my uncle and aunt. Much to my horror, unexpected circumstances meant they left me hosting their 'very religious friends'. I prepared myself for the worst, but to this day I have never forgotten the moment I first saw Lynn and Marti Green and their daughter Sharon. There was something about the way they interacted that was like nothing I had ever seen before. Their interactions were marked by love, joy and peace. Even more extraordinary was the way they spoke about Jesus, like he was alive and with us and that he had purpose for our lives. Something in me wanted what they had; if that had something to do with this man Jesus, I was determined to find out. They gave me a Bible and I began to explore for myself who Jesus was.

I was like ripe fruit waiting to be picked when on Remembrance Sunday, 14 November 1999, I turned up at Holy Trinity Brompton in London. Sandy Millar powerfully proclaimed the truth of Jesus and the God who is good and who will defeat all evil. At the end an invitation was given for those who wanted to give their today for the sake of the next generation's tomorrow. I found myself standing; my surrender to Jesus was complete. Everything changed. That was demonstrated when, out clubbing with friends a week or so later, I was offered some coke. My simple unrehearsed response spontaneously declared what was utterly true: 'No thanks! I feel so free!' I had found freedom and life because of Jesus.

By this time I had moved to London and had fallen into event management and subsequently design production at a small legal magazine. An old family friend, who was serving with Jackie Pullinger-To in Hong Kong and had been sent to start a work in another south-east Asian country, invited me to go and see her in 2002. During my two weeks there we took rice boxes to the street children at the train station. As I sat on the floor of the station a thought thundered through me: 'The people you don't see are the people that matter to me!' In an instant I remembered a time a few years earlier, in 1995, when I had been in this station while making my way west of the big bustling Asian metropolis.

Travelling with friends, we had been trying to get off the well-trodden tourist path and find a more authentic and real experience. Ending up on the border, we'd gone out in rowing boats and found ourselves near a very small floating house. The three men within it had beckoned us to join them. As we sat drinking whisky, they'd pointed to the distant hills and explained that was their nation and that they were living in exile. They began to tell us of the suffering of their people. Over the next three days, they showed us undercover footage of different aspects of life in their home nation. (I'm deliberately not naming this country because of the sensitive situation there, given its anti-gospel stance.) Before I left, they'd come to the balcony of the hostel where I was staying and given me a wooden carving. They said they gave these to people 'who would do something for their people, for their nation' and then asked if I would do something for them. My reply had been quick and emphatic: 'Yes.'

On my return to university, I'd written, spoken and lobbied politically for their nation and these people. I knew that my time with those men had been deeply significant; I felt then something that I had never experienced before. The moment they asked me to help them, I'd had a tangible sense of someone's presence, which I came to understand was the presence of God. So having returned to the train station in 2002 where this memory resurfaced within me, I sat scribbling again and again this long-forgotten and often unseen nation's name on a piece of paper.

Back in the UK after this trip, I ended up training as a teacher, but from the outset I knew that my yes to Jesus would look quite different to working full-time in a school. The training became a means by which I could earn enough money to live; the rest of the time I gave to my local church – I had joined a wonderful church-planting movement in south-east London which I am part of to this day – while all the time carrying the memory of the promise I had given on that balcony in south-east Asia. On New Year's Eve 2004, I was praying and fasting and preparing to write a study paper on John 8:12 where Jesus says, 'I am the light of the world. Whoever follows me will never walk in darkness, but will have the light of life.' Suddenly I heard the still small voice of Jesus. He was inviting me to honour the yes I had given those men and do something, but it was not to be about politics! My focus was to be his light, his kingdom and his love! So began my journey.

Mission in south-east Asia

My mission started small and for many years I would come and go. On my first trip in 2005 I travelled with an eighty-three-year-old lady but I knew no one there. While on my knees in the hotel room, asking the Holy Spirit to help me, the phone rang. Someone was in the lobby inviting me to a birthday party. It was hardly the kind of thing I wanted to be doing, but it was the only door of opportunity I had. So I went and then met a wonderful brother in the faith who had a ministry with drug addicts.

He invited me to visit his rehabilitation centre, where I also met a younger sister serving in his ministry.

Over the coming years, I continued to partner with this brother but didn't reconnect with the younger sister until 2011. She had a vision for the children of the nation and a passion for Jesus that led her to do many exploits with God. One of these was an annual camp for hundreds of kids, which I went to visit. Sitting down together, she asked me to help her. We began a conversation about what it would be like to partner together rather than operating using the model of dependency that so often dominates modern missions. I could see her gifting, anointing and calling, and I did not want local initiative stifled. We developed a training course for those who wanted to lead children's ministry.

As I prepped for this, I knew I was imparting a fresh vision for the local church and also challenging people with their own personal discipleship – you can't lead children where you haven't been yourself in relationship with the Holy Spirit. No more than ten people turned up the first time we ran the course in July 2012, and I remember feeling a little grumpy before the Lord! Yet in his kindness he encouraged me not to despise the day of small beginnings. Now, in 2024, I am still working with some of these people, who have become some of our most significant leaders today. Everything that has been birthed stems from that first training course!

Back to 2012, by the end of the week of running that course, my local friend told me she knew she had to start a church in her house and did I want to join them? I am amazed to this day that I simply said no! But, despite this, the fellowship started. Thereafter, every time I visited and shared time or training with them, I could see the Holy Spirit was birthing something really special. By March 2014, local friends started asking me when I was going to move and live in the region. In September 2014, I finally turned up with a couple of bags knowing one thing: I wanted to be a permanent part of what God was doing among my friends and in that fellowship!

The calibre of these people that I began sharing life with, day in and day out, was humbling. The friend who I had developed the training course with had become my cultural mentor, and together we began to lead the ministry. She came from a remote region in the north, where she'd come to know Jesus and had certainly seen for herself his extraordinary power. Calling herself a jungle woman, she found herself in the same big city as me for one thing: Jesus! So me, a posh girl (my time at a top boarding school was part of a really privileged upbringing), and this jungle woman joined forces to enter a new and exciting phase. Our fellowship continued, as did the annual kids' camp, but I longed for us to do more to reach the working kids and the street kids.

A trip to the cinema became the event that really changed the shape of who we were. In 2015, as all the team that had led at that annual kids' camp came out of the cinema, we stopped to take a selfie and found ourselves surrounded by a bunch of street children photobombing us. A few days later, as our core team met to pray and fast, one of the team suggested we take rice boxes to those children. And so began our weekly pavement picnic. It was a long-held dream of mine to be out on the street in this way reaching the working and homeless children. However, I never wanted to lead something unless there was a consensus among us in case one day I was kicked out of the country. I felt deeply that whatever we did needed to be owned across the team so it would continue without relying on me. And now it was actually happening!

The Holy Spirit had again birthed something and it was beautiful. The team shook off their fear and long-held beliefs about outreach to engage in friendship, play and prayer with all the kids and those from the street community who came. We began to share about Jesus. We saw children put their bags down and play; we saw hard hearts melt and receive hugs; we saw miracles of healing. They were wonderful years of boldness! This had been a closed country, but now it was opening up, and our team were being so courageous. Many laughed at us and did not understand our convictions, but we persisted. As we did, we met the ones on the street who had no family.

The Joy Centre

One such boy came every week. Like so many street children, problems began at home after his father died. His mother started a new relationship and his stepfather abused him. His mother then put him and his brother in a monastery, but here too they were abused, so they both ran away to the city. After a few days' journey, they arrived safely, but at some point in those first days he told us he lost his younger brother. This boy would come every week to our pavement picnic and was a catalyst for the vision that was stirring within us. In 2016 he decided he no longer wanted to be on the street and wanted to be a family with us. So he would stay with my friend and also come and stay with me in my one-bedroom apartment in a market community. All the challenges of what it means to love, serve and do family in a meaningful way with street children happened. He would settle. He would run. In the midst of all of this, we felt the Holy Spirit give us a vision of a home where we could all live together: me, my friend, her two birth children and any other children the Lord would send us. We even had the name: it would be called the Joy Centre family after that part of a baby's brain where the emotions of joy and delight are felt when it is smiled over and held by its parents.

Gender inequality, poverty, child abuse, child labour and human trafficking block so many children's chance of a childhood. Here one in five children have no education. Over one third of the children are estimated to be working. Ten children die every hour and many children are abandoned at birth. Yet children are precious and a priority to our Father God, so they are to us too! We would be a kingdom family where children would have a sense of belonging, significance, security, acceptance, love, praise and discipline. We wanted to provide an opportunity to rest, play, create and learn in a safe and loving environment because that is the family environment.

Like children we were dreaming big! The vision was clear and the Holy Spirit spoke clearly to me to begin to design the architectural plans for the Joy Centre family building. Confirmation to take this step came through a prophetic word from my church in the UK. So, still with no financial resources, I got a builder friend to draw up plans. We went and looked at land. When slowly but surely the finances came in, we could rent our first house. The dream remains to buy land and build a centre, but for these last six years we have continued to rent.

We were set to move in and start the Joy Centre family on 1 May 2018, and in the meantime were praying and fasting. Days before the move, I was woken with this thought thundering through my innermost being: 'Many thousands will be baptised in the name of the Father, Son and Holy Spirit. They will be kick-started in their identity as sons and daughters of the Living God.' Like David in 2 Samuel 7:8–17, I found my voice and prayed this crazy bold and courageous prayer back to God. I had never felt so much of his pleasure on a prayer before. In that moment I knew that what we were doing in establishing the Joy Centre family embodied the spirit of adoption that is in the heart of the Father and that is beating over this nation.

When 1 May actually came, our first son had run away, so my friend and I were somewhat discouraged. But within two days of starting the Joy Centre family, at our weekly pavement picnic, a precious daughter decided to come home. This is her story. Despite now being baptised and filled with the Holy Spirit, she has dark and difficult days and still struggles to open up about her past. At these times the pressure of being in family can become too much for her and she runs. On one occasion, within a few hours of leaving home, someone she had trusted had given her to two men, who ultimately sold her into the sex industry. Having slept the night in a madam's house, she was woken and then dressed in clothes that made it very clear to her what was about to happen. She was then left in a hotel room, where a pot-bellied and naked policeman entered. Our daughter knew the one thing to do in that moment and she called on the name of Jesus. To this day we are not totally clear how, but something supernatural happened and she was able to flee the room and escape. Someone gave her enough money to get a bus home. When she eventually returned, we were all in awe of what God had done. Yet again we had seen the simple truth that if you call on the name of Jesus, he moves. We have seen this time and again over the years.

One lady in my old market community had suffered from chronic pain for over fifteen years. We prayed for her healing and then sent her on her way with the name of Jesus. We simply said that when the pain was particularly acute, she should call on Jesus. Twelve months later, this lady was smiling from ear to ear and could not contain her excitement. She had done as we said and continued to call on Jesus, and all her pain was gone. Another friend of ours from the street community was recently faced with having to give her son to the military. She did not want him forcefully conscripted and remembered what we had always said to her about calling on the name of Jesus. In that moment she called on Jesus to hide and protect her son, and he was not taken. When she saw us again, she recounted how, after asking Jesus to help, her son was spared. Aunty Shout is a friend who spends her days sweeping up human and dog faeces at the main station in the city. She is another who has heard our encouragement many times. One day her daughter, unable to swim, fell into deep water. Aunty called on the name of Jesus and somehow her daughter came to the surface fighting for her breath. To this day she repeats this testimony every time we see her. Living on the train platform, she starts and ends her days talking to Jesus.

Our Joy Centre family has grown and there are now nine children. The two eldest sons have been wonderfully restored to their birth families. One of these is our first son who had run away just before we started the Joy Centre family in 2018. After ending up back on the street and having been sold into labour, he was pushed into working for one of the many fishing businesses operating in the region. He'd realised what was happening and remembered what we'd always told him: if you get stuck in a situation and you don't know what to do, call on the name of Jesus. He did that and then courageously escaped from the hotel where he was sleeping in the early hours of the morning. A man helped him and lent him a phone to call us. It was 3 a.m. With no car, we rallied a friend who has a taxi and set off to rescue him. This became a catalyst in his life and he not only got a job but has been wonderfully reconciled to his mother and step-father. We even managed to find his younger brother! The remaining seven children keep us very busy. The youngest is eighteen months and the eldest eighteen years.

Trusting our faithful God in the face of trials

The core team loving and serving both the Joy Centre vision and the Street Church vision is now eight adults. I am so thankful for this community and family that loves extravagantly. I am also extremely grateful for the fact that we stand together in all things, expectant that we will see God's goodness in our lives and in the land where we are living. The last years have brought many trials and challenges after military rule was re-established, changing everything overnight. Yet we have learnt that no matter what happens, we will live unafraid. Even should the worst happen, we have Jesus and the abundance of his life and freedom that can never be taken from us! We have also learnt that everything we face brings increased revelation of the depth and power and truth of the gospel. We do not need to shrink the gospel so it fits what we are experiencing. What we are doing matters, and things that matter are hard. In the same way that gold and silver are refined by fire, Jesus purifies our hearts through tests and trials. So why are we surprised when things get really hot and intense? There is constant uncertainty living in a place like this and the challenges are real. Whether they are the challenges of language and culture or what is happening on the wider scene across the nation, there are ever-present obstacles and dangers.

Many friends have fled the country, and many others of us have been scattered across this nation and neighbouring nations. Other friends have been imprisoned, and I have witnessed evil on a scale I could never have imagined. Voices all around me have told me to get out and to leave. I don't know how to explain it to people, but I have felt no such conviction. I remember going swimming once when it began to rain. I thought to myself, 'I should get out, it's raining.' That was a ridiculous thought considering I was utterly soaked already! And, quick as a flash, the Holy Spirit convicted me with great humour saying, 'That is as ridiculous as saying you should leave this country! You have already died. You don't need to leave for fear of what might happen.'

So I keep going, keep putting to death my worldly ambitions, and keep growing in my obedience to God. I keep worshipping him, keep taking the journey he is leading me on and keep experiencing the goodness of the Father.

I know he is faithful and so I will continue to give my yes.

If you would like more information about Sarah's work or to get in touch with her, please email: hello@greatlakesoutreach.org

3

DUNCAN DYASON

GUATEMALA

Blackpool, England – 1981

The 1980s were a whirlwind of social and political upheaval, and technological innovation. Yet, amid this sea of change, I was adrift, grappling to find purpose in what felt like a void of meaning.

At just twenty-one, I felt my journey had reached its bleak conclusion. One day, I arrived home burdened with the means to end my seemingly pointless, sad, lonely life. As I flopped onto my bed, bracing myself for what would come, a thought pierced my mind: 'What happens when I die?' The profound longing in my soul for meaning drove me to cry out, 'God, if you are there, help me!'

I knew I was alone, yet was surprised by an audible voice: 'Go to Tunbridge Wells and seek me there.' I immediately sat up, startled, and felt a strange comfort, a simple faith settling over me. This was God speaking to me – a God I had never believed in, now calling me on a journey that would change my life forever. My mind buzzed with newfound hope.

Early the following day, I informed my employer of my plans and bought a one-way train ticket to Tunbridge Wells, Kent. Upon arriving mid-afternoon, my excitement began to morph into anxiety. I had no place to sleep that night or means of supporting myself. Yet, as I wandered up from the station, I noticed an advertisement for a bedsit in the window of a newsagent. Contacting the owners, I was told that it would be mine if I could find employment in the remaining two working hours of the day – a seemingly impossible task.

The advisor at the job centre, upon learning of my lack of qualifications and an address, bluntly suggested I return to Blackpool. Determined, I crossed the road to a large department store, where a man approached me with an unexpected question: 'Looking for a job?' He needed someone to sell silverware and, despite my lack of retail experience, invited me to 'Give it a try.' My would-be landlords were speechless by my story and handed me the key with a smile.

Sunday arrived soon enough, and with no work to occupy my time, I lounged in bed, pondering how to spend the day. The ringing bells interrupted my thoughts, and I quickly realised they were church bells. The idea struck me: 'That's where God lives.' I had experienced God speaking to me, and now I wanted to go to church and thank him. The experience was confusing as I had no idea when to sit or stand, or which book to use, but there was something profoundly moving about being there.

Over the next three weeks, I was captivated by what I continued to learn at church, but it all seemed like a lot of complex information, particularly why Jesus died on the cross. I could not fully comprehend what this meant for me until I was desperately trying to work a tiny portable TV I had bought from a colleague at work. The strongest signal was for BBC1, on which the film *Ben Hur* had just begun.

As I watched, another character seized my attention. Set during the life of Jesus, the film portrayed his crucifixion in graphic detail. Despite hearing about Jesus dying for my sins in church, it wasn't until that poignant moment, with him nailed to the cross, his gaze falling upon the cheering crowd, that the depth of his forgiveness stirred my spirit.

A light had been switched on in my head, and I understood. Jesus loved me. The truth of his grace and redemption impacted me so much that I fell to my knees, tears streaming down my face in torrents. Each tear felt like a confession, a testament to the weight of my past transgressions – the years of teenage rebellion, the destructive choices and the rejection of God's lordship over my life. With every sob, I called out to God, pleading for his forgiveness.

The following morning, it felt like a burden had been lifted from my soul. As I left for work, the world unfurled before my eyes in brilliant detail – trees, flowers and plants had a newfound vibrancy. It was as if I had been given new eyes, enabling me to see God's creation in all its glory. I was enveloped by an undeniable truth: God's love had claimed me, and my journey henceforth was dedicated to his divine purpose.

I started assisting with the church youth group, then soon the minister encouraged me to consider a path towards full-time Christian ministry. Those were exhilarating days as I witnessed God's mighty hand at work within and around me. He reshaped my desires, transformed my thinking and continually revealed the depth of his love and forgiveness for me.

In the late summer of 1984, just three years after surrendering my life to Christ, I embarked on a transformative journey at Moorlands Bible College, enrolling in a three-year course on theology and youth work. My closest friend was Simon Lang, who came from a Christian family with roots deeply entrenched in the African mission field. His captivating tales of serving God across continents and enthusiasm inspired us to volunteer for a memorable venture: providing transport to Poland during the summer break for two female students.

Poland – 1985

Unfamiliar with life in Poland but eager to spend time with the two enchanting Polish students who fervently sought our help, Simon and I agreed to assist with their summer outreach mission in northern Poland. As our plans took shape, it quickly became apparent that our task was far more extensive than we thought – it expanded into volunteering with a summer camp for children and securing medical supplies for a hospital, essential food items and Bibles. This meant we needed a larger vehicle and a reliable fundraising method. Without a charitable framework or a dedicated supporter network, we found ourselves turning to the most powerful resource available to us: prayer.

Our journey took an astonishing turn when a Christian magazine published an article about our upcoming mission. This caught the attention of Brother Andrew, the legendary Dutch missionary known for smuggling Bibles to churches behind the Iron Curtain. He generously offered us a substantial supply of Bibles, which he said we could collect from him en route to Poland. Meanwhile, God was touching hearts and donations began to pour in, allowing us to procure medical supplies, canned food, Sunday School materials and delightful treats for the children. Miraculously, our needs were met fully, including acquiring a sturdy Land Rover generously outfitted with a large roof rack to carry our expanding cargo.

At 4 a.m. on the appointed July morning, we were brimming with excitement as we packed our personal belongings into the Land Rover, ready to embark on our mission to Poland. My exhilaration at being part of this mission seemed infectious, uplifting Simon and our two Polish companions as we sailed towards an adventure that promised so much.

By late afternoon, we found ourselves at a layby on the outskirts of Eindhoven. Seeking respite from the intense sun, we gathered under the shade of a majestic elm tree as we eagerly awaited the spirited Dutch missionary's arrival. An old grey Volvo estate finally pulled into the layby and a middle-aged man emerged, his presence exuding a quiet energy.

We exchanged warm greetings with Brother Andrew and proudly showcased the Land Rover, brimming with supplies destined for the church in Warsaw. Brother Andrew's eyes sparkled with joy as he saw the ample space on the roof rack for the precious Bibles. Soon thirty boxes of Bibles were carefully loaded onto the Land Rover, secured tightly with rope and a blue tarpaulin. Brother Andrew listened intently as we recounted how the Lord had guided us to this moment. He prayed for our mission, especially for our safety as we prepared to cross the Iron Curtain, and requested that we keep him updated on our progress. His blessings and enthusiasm infused us with renewed confidence and purpose.

I had read numerous accounts of courageous Christians who devoted their lives to aiding the persecuted church in East Germany and Poland, and the gravity of their experiences began to sink in. The thought of navigating through the formidable checkpoints of the Iron Curtain now seemed far more daunting than I had initially assumed.

Having travelled through the heart of West Germany, we eventually found ourselves at the border with East

Germany. There, we applied for a permit to traverse the corridor leading to the checkpoint near Rzepin, Poland. As we drew closer, the sight of a long queue of vans, cars and lorries stirred a wave of anxiety within me. The vehicles ahead were being subjected to meticulous searches, heightening my apprehension. Sensing our unease, our charming Polish companions revealed a troubling fact: the Polish authorities were looking for banned items, such as Bibles and medical supplies, unless accompanied by specific written permission. The revelation left me taken aback. At that moment, there was little else we could do but turn our hearts to prayer, entrusting everything to God's sovereign control.

A stern-faced guard motioned us forward as we rolled up to the checkpoint. His steely demeanour suggested years of experience and an acute awareness of every possible ploy used to smuggle prohibited items into the country. He tapped on the window, and as I lowered it, he demanded our passports, his eyes scanning the interior of the Land Rover with rigorous scrutiny.

'What do you have in the vehicle?' he inquired.

'Well, mainly,' I responded with a hint of irony, 'we are carrying Bibles and medical supplies.'

The guard glanced at me, his stern expression softening into an unexpected smile as he handed back the two British and two Polish passports.

'You British are so funny,' he said.

He then casually gestured for us to take the exit lane and continue our journey. It felt almost miraculous and incredibly humorous – God's providence had seen us through this tense moment, allowing us to pass without a hitch.

By the time we arrived at the Baptist church in Warsaw, it was nearly 8 p.m. Exhausted from the long journey yet elated by our safe arrival, we were warmly greeted by the church pastor. He invited us to a special dinner prepared in the church's basement by one of the families in the church. The sight that met our eyes was nothing short of astounding – a lavish spread of Polish soup, assorted cheeses, hams, sauces and fresh bread. Midway through my meal, a sudden thought struck me: 'Where did all this food come from?' Considering the well-known food shortages in Poland, it puzzled me how one family could manage to provide such an abundant feast.

I confided to Simon my concerns, wondering aloud if we had been misled into bringing basic food supplies when there appeared to be plenty. Our Polish friends, noticing our whispered conversation, inquired about what we were discussing. Unable to hold back, I candidly expressed my frustration – how their stories of people living in poverty contrasted sharply with the generous feast provided by a single family.

As Iwona, one of the Polish students, spoke, her eyes welled with tears. She explained how this family was so excited by our visit that they had sacrificed their own sustenance for many days to prepare this single meal for us. The mother had even spent four hours queuing just to get the meat! It was a profoundly humbling experience, setting the tone for all that we were to encounter over the following two weeks.

That first missionary experience in Poland changed my life. I was challenged in so many ways, particularly to examine everything in my heart that was not right before God, and was now ready to give my life to mission.

Chesham Bois, England – 1987

After completing three enriching years at Moorlands Bible College, I married Jenni and accepted the youth worker role at an Anglican church in the picturesque village of Chesham Bois, Buckinghamshire. This marked the beginning of yet another thrilling chapter in my life. My fervour to reach young people with the good news of God's love fuelled a series of new outreach initiatives. I began to engage local schools, opened youth clubs and organised various youth events within the community.

We were filled with joy as my fourth year as a youth worker coincided with the birth of our beautiful daughter, Katelyn. Our hearts were excited, dreaming of creating a warm, loving home and expanding our youth ministry. One Sunday evening, after returning home from a lively youth group session, I was tired and drained, longing for my bed. Yet, my mind buzzed with the evening's activities, making it hard to wind down. I settled down with a cup of hot tea and turned on the TV. Just then, a BBC *Everyman* programme began, titled 'They Shoot Children, Don't They?' It featured a charity's work with an estimated 5,000 street children in Guatemala City, Guatemala.

I had never heard of Guatemala, nor was I aware that thousands of children lived on the streets and were being hunted down by police, tortured and killed. The documentary was harrowing and left an indelible mark on my heart. Deeply moved, I couldn't shake the images from my mind. The next day, I recounted what I had seen to Jenni and expressed how my heart was irresistibly drawn towards working with these vulnerable children.

Jenni was taken aback, and we both agreed that we needed divine confirmation to ensure this calling was from God and not merely an emotional response to the documentary. Yet, we recalled attending a conference in the north of England the previous December, where a woman we had never met approached us. With unwavering confidence, she declared that God was calling us to serve in another country and that I was to be 'a father to the fatherless'. She exhorted, 'When the time is right, God will open the doors. Pray for open doors.' Her words now echoed in our minds, reinforcing our sense of purpose and direction.

My boss and our minister, Rev. Mike Hill, invited me to a meeting the following day. He shared that God had spoken to him many months earlier, urging the church to prepare for our eventual departure to serve in mission work abroad. As if this revelation wasn't astonishing enough, I received a phone call from a friend that same day asking to meet me. He confided that God had placed something on his heart – to offer his free time to support us, sensing that we might one day be called to serve in mission.

These affirmations, coming in swift succession, felt nothing short of miraculous. In August 1992, we bade farewell to the UK and set off for Guatemala.

Guatemala – 1992

Upon our arrival in Guatemala, we immediately began our language training, immersing ourselves in the new culture. I started working as a street outreach worker while Jenni stayed home to care for Katelyn. Unfortunately, the organisation we had come to serve with closed its doors soon after we arrived. Having travelled such a long way and sacrificed so much to be there, we were left in a state of uncertainty. We earnestly prayed to God, seeking his guidance on the next steps he wanted us to take.

Our call was as strong as ever, despite attempts to take my life or to kidnap our daughter. These were challenging times, but we knew God would open the doors and show us how his heart for the children on the streets would lead many to know and serve him.

Over the years, the ministry flourished, and the number of children living on the streets dwindled. The violence against these vulnerable youngsters was greatly reduced, prompting significant reforms within the Guatemalan social services departments.

During this transformative period, I focused on developing a mentoring programme specifically for children living on the streets and those at high risk of ending up there. This initiative became one of our many strategies to reach and support more vulnerable children.

However, our efforts soon highlighted a pressing need: we required a permanent base – a centre that could serve as a hub for our mentoring activities and potentially as a refuge for the children.

Despite not having any money for a building, I met with our team of volunteers and explained to them the need and my desire that the centre be in the heart of where we worked. I invited them to join me in prayer. Then, in faith, I reached out to an estate agent, who showed me an interesting property close to La Terminal, a huge market area in Guatemala City where we worked daily.

The property was a dilapidated warehouse that had stood abandoned for over two years. Massive holes in the roof allowed rainwater to flood inside, and the place was infested with rats. Nevertheless, we inquired about the price and were told it was on offer for $150,000. While not the cheapest option in the city, its size and proximity to La Terminal, where property prices were surprisingly high, made it a valuable asset. We informed the estate agent of our strong interest and assured him that we would pray about securing the necessary funds.

Later that day, I attended our evening service at Vida Real, a vibrant and fast-growing evangelical church in Guatemala City that was known as a beacon of faith in the community. However, as I walked into the service, I felt the Lord impress upon me that I needed to prepare myself to go up on stage. This filled me with anxiety, as being in front of people is one of my least favourite things. My apprehension grew so intense that I eventually left the service and headed to the bathroom, thinking I might be sick. I tried to reassure myself with reason: in all my years attending Vida Real, no one had ever been randomly called up on stage.

When I returned to the auditorium, the time of lively worship had concluded and a lady stood on stage, scanning the congregation. My pastor, Rony Madrid, noticed me walking back in. With a microphone in hand, he exclaimed, 'He's the one!' and beckoned me forward. Confused and nervous, I took the microphone and joined the lady on stage. She then announced that the Lord wished to encourage me: 'The horizon is your vision. God is only limited by your faith in him. Do not worry about the provision; God will provide for your plans, and your heart will lead many to him.' Her words resonated deeply, filling me with a mix of awe and reassurance. After she prayed for me, I returned to my seat, my mind swirling with thoughts about all that the Lord was orchestrating in my life.

The following day, I was working with our street team on 5th Avenue in La Terminal and passed by the Hotel Felicidad (Hotel Happiness), one of the many brothels in the area. I noticed a man sitting on the pavement outside the entrance. He wore dark-brown leather boots, jeans, a dark hoodie and a baseball cap that obscured his eyes. Suddenly, he looked up at me and beckoned me to come closer. Cautiously, I leaned forward, and he gently pulled my head towards his mouth as if to share a secret. He said,

'The blessing of God is coming for you; it will be much bigger than you can ever imagine, but God will keep you safe. Just trust in him.'

I stepped back, lost for words, and turned to find one of the team members working with me. I spotted one a few metres down the road, playing with some of the children. As I walked over, he noticed my shocked expression and asked if everything was okay. I pointed back to where the man had been sitting, ready to recount the strange encounter, but to my surprise, the man was nowhere to be seen.

Later, our team gathered to pray about the day's events. We felt a profound sense that God was affirming his promise to provide for the mentoring centre. The mysterious encounter strengthened our trust in his divine provision and guidance.

The next day, our friendly estate agent called to inform me that the owner would drop the price to $140,000 if we could secure a deal in the coming days. I reiterated to him that we were expectant that God would provide and that we would be in touch soon.

A few hours later, my phone rang, and I saw on the screen that it was an Amersham number. Answering, I was surprised by the voice of a friend I hadn't heard from in over a year – Jonathan Harbottle. After exchanging warm greetings, Jonathan told me that he and his wife, Ana Maria, had been thinking about ways they could support our ministry. Although they knew little about my current work in Guatemala, they wanted to share their idea.

Jonathan revealed that if we ever needed a building as a base, they were willing to invest in a property that could help towards their pension. We could use the building freely until it was no longer needed, at which point it would be sold and the funds would return to them. I couldn't help but laugh, taken aback by the perfect timing. When Jonathan was curious about my reaction, I shared how we felt the Lord was leading us to purchase and transform a dilapidated warehouse into a mentoring centre.

Jonathan received the plan warmly but quickly clarified that they didn't have a huge sum of money available. What they could offer, however, was $140,000! Overjoyed, I thanked him and Ana Maria profusely. Without wasting a moment, I called the estate agent to finalise the property purchase. God had indeed spoken – he had promised to provide for his work, and now he had demonstrated his faithfulness extraordinarily.

The following week, we left the mentoring centre and set out for La Terminal, ready to embark on another afternoon's work. We passed the familiar faces of street youths, all high on solvents. Arriving once again at the notorious Hotel Felicidad, we exchanged greetings with the manager and the mothers lingering outside, each vying to lure new clients within. Swiftly, we transformed a small patch of the street into a makeshift school, where the fortunate few attending school could unpack their bags and dive into their homework with our guidance. Heavy with the promise of the rainy season, the dark sky loomed overhead, reminding us that our efforts might be cut short by a sudden downpour.

It wasn't long before a strong, cold wind blew in from the north, prompting people to seek cover and hurriedly dismantle or cover their market stalls. I approached the hotel manager to ask if there was an empty room we could use to shelter and support the children with homework until the storm passed. Graciously, we were offered free use of a large, empty room on the third floor. We gathered our belongings and the children, crossed the hotel's courtyard and climbed the steps to the top floor. Brimming with anticipation, the children raced ahead, their laughter echoing up the stairwell.

We quickly transformed the space into a makeshift classroom, guiding the children through lessons and playful games. The session culminated with a lively demonstration of the proper tooth-brushing techniques! Miraculously, just as we finished, the rain ceased and the sun broke through the clouds, casting its unique orange glow over the courtyard. The children, their eyes gleaming with renewed energy and ready to play in the warm sunshine, eagerly asked if we could return to the street below.

As we gathered our materials, the children dashed down the stairs joyfully, their school bags clattering against the metal railings like a cascade of notes. Following them, I paused at the doorway and caught sight of a man across the corridor leaning against the third-floor railing. He straightened up and motioned for me to approach. While the rest of the team squeezed past, eager to return to the now sunny street below, I walked along the corridor and greeted the man with a cautious hello, extending my hand.

Although physically shorter, his presence unsettled me. As he leaned in uncomfortably close, a shiver ran down my spine – I immediately sensed that something was terribly wrong. An uneasy silence hung in the air. His dark eyes exuded a malevolent intensity that sent waves of dread through me.

By now his face was mere inches from mine.

My heart pounded in my chest as he drew a gun from the front of his jeans.

'I'm going to kill you,' he hissed, his eyes ablaze with malice. His words sent a chill through my bones.

A thought entered my mind and I replied, 'Why do you want to kill me?'

With disgust in his voice, the man rambled on about his suspicions about me and my work with the children, saying, 'I know you steal children and take them to your country.' He continued asking me, 'What do you do with them when you get there? Do you remove their organs?'

This man was very confused about what the team and I were doing in La Terminal, but it seemed unlikely that he would believe my rebuttal.

So I said, 'If you are going to kill me, I would like one minute of your time.' Without waiting for his reply, I stood up a little and began to recount, as fast as I could, my testimony of how God had changed my life and how the man, like I had done, could put his trust in Jesus. I have never squeezed so much information about the saving work of Christ in such a small amount of time.

Though it felt like an eternity, I took a breath and looked at the man. I could see that my story had made some impact on him. His hardened gaze softened, and his eyes were now looking down at the floor rather than burrowing into mine. He looked back at me and said, 'Well, that answers my question.'

He recounted how he had spotted me at Hotel Felicidad the previous week. As the team and I left the building, he watched with keen eyes as we exchanged goodbyes and I then turned right into a small side street. He followed me, describing accurately how I turned left at the end of the street and then right before entering a dark alley where my car was parked.

With a chilling calmness, he revealed that he had then drawn his gun, tapping it now in the palm of his hand for emphasis. He had aimed it at me and squeezed the trigger. To his utter shock, the gun didn't fire. He tried again, first attempting to shoot me in the head, and when that failed, aiming at my back. Both times, the gun refused to discharge.

He explained that he was one of 'Los Angeles' (local contract killers) and used the weapon almost daily. It had never once failed him in all the years he had owned the gun. 'Now I know why my gun failed,' he admitted. 'It is because God is with you.'

I stood there, speechless and reeling, struggling to comprehend the gravity of his words, as I felt my heart pounding hard inside my chest. Carefully, the man placed the gun back into his jeans and extended his right hand. 'My name is Luis,' he said. As if by instinct, I shook his hand – the hand of someone who had not only tried to kill me the previous week but had also threatened to finish the job that very day.

Before I could gather my thoughts in the wake of Luis's declaration, he spoke again. 'From now on, I will be watching your back,' he said with a newfound trust.

A hesitant smile tugged at my lips as I asked, 'In a good way?'

Luis's laughter echoed down the corridor, a surprisingly warm sound. He reached out and touched my shoulder, a gesture that spoke volumes. He guided me towards the steps with gentle pressure, and we exchanged farewells.

Stepping out into the bustling street, I stood next to one of our team members, who cradled a small child in her arms, providing much-needed comfort. 'Shall we go?' I asked, attempting to return to normalcy as we headed back to the mentoring centre. Though the day's events remained at the forefront of my mind, I could not speak about what had just transpired. Only on returning home did the reality hit me and bring me to tears. Once again, God had fulfilled his promise, and I extended my arms in praise.

Our ministry flourished as the favour of the Lord rested upon us all. We witnessed God transforming lives and turning around the most seemingly impossible situations. Within our dedicated team, a spirit of unity and enthusiasm permeated all we did as we worked together to transform the dilapidated warehouse into a safe, well-equipped centre. 'El Centro' (The Centre) became an incredible place of belonging for the children, offering them hope and refuge. God's presence was unmistakable, and we continued to see his glory revealed through the countless lives being changed around us.

Reflections – 2024

I consider myself the most unlikely of Christians. My conversion to Christ continually reminds me that my life is his and that I can only achieve what he empowers me to do. Fully understanding that we are saved by grace places the indelible fingerprint of God on everything we undertake. I know I am called to trust him and to put that trust into action. As I do so, I witness God, who created and sustains the universe, guiding my hand and blessing my life. However, God does not promise a life free from hardship. Instead, he assures us of his steadfast presence, helping us find purpose through our trials.

There is a hurting world around us, desperate to know these truths and witness God's love and power firsthand. In sharing these stories, I hope you will find encouragement and blessing. I pray that God will remind you of how deeply you are loved and reveal his purpose for your life. One certainty remains: God will never leave you alone nor abandon you. His purposes will always be revealed if we take the time to listen, trust and then act. Enjoy the journey!

4

ALLI BLAIR

THAILAND TO CAMBODIA VIA AFRICA

A visiting friend asked my mother her secret of child-raising, on hearing that all four Blair siblings – aged twelve to twenty-five – were in different countries at the time. After a moment's reflection, my mother replied, 'Affectionate neglect!'

Born in England, four months after the Queen's coronation, I grew up between Quebec, Canada and Kent with loving, creative parents, who were quick to laugh and encourage our many projects. Dad espoused vintage cars and woodworking; Mum music, painting and outsize papier mâché; we kids rejoiced in summer camping and winter skiing, climbing trees, digging to Australia and rescuing animals – all interspersed with boats and voracious reading.

The nos and the yeses: Kent, England – 1972

At home alone in bed one night, with a stub of pencil and a tiny notebook – one should never be without a tiny notebook – I drew a line down the middle of the page and put God in the dock. *Yes* or *No*? *No* because everything is forbidden once you become a Christian. *No* because Christians are all boring. *No* because how can I believe if I don't believe? The *No*s were tumbling off the page when I heard, 'I AM.' All my flimsy arguments melted away and suddenly everything became simple and obvious: *God is*. What a glorious relief! I just let go of my doubts, and only then understood my darkness beside God's holiness. Immediately I then had a picture of someone filling up my darkness with liquid light, which I understood was Jesus cleaning out my darkness and filling my heart with song. And that was the beginning of my salvation. But accepting Jesus' lordship was another story.

Prepare ye the way: Canada – 1972

While at Laval University in Quebec, Canada, I was playing truant one winter day and planning to ski. Praying first, suddenly a huge photograph filled the sunny wall of my little apartment. It was of an isolated rural path with the caption, 'Prepare ye the way' (Matthew 3:3, KJV). After that, a friend gave me a book, *The Latent Power of the Soul* by Watchman Nee, that transformed my understanding of Christianity. With a shocking bolt of lightning, I finally realised that God wanted me for himself all day, every day and on his terms, not mine. He was to be Lord! My nice arrangement of tuning in to God when or if it suited me was an aberration to be repented of and abandoned immediately. This marked the beginning of a relationship with the only One who can ever bring fulfilment.

The decisive carving knife: Great Yarmouth, England – 1978-79

In 1978, after university, I was living in an old Great Yarmouth rectory that had been converted into a Christian community offering shelter to severely disturbed adults and adolescents. One day, in the kitchen, my co-worker Ruth's bread was rising when suddenly Roger, one of the residents, changed my destiny by attacking me with a carving knife. I shielded myself by wielding a solid Norfolk chair and lived to tell the tale. The incident sent me on to theological college – St John's College, Nottingham – to seek answers to the many questions accumulated while working with the deeply wounded.

There, in 1980, while gathered around the television in our very comfortable common room, suddenly, unexpectedly, we were stabbed by unimaginable images of the Killing Fields of Cambodia – stark skeletal human beings with dark living-dead eyes, living in the horrors of hell. Our theological training was all very well, but I needed to know, *Was God really there?* After finishing college, I finally got visa and paperwork in order to work with Christian Outreach (COR) in the Thailand-based refugee camps for survivors of the genocide. I flew to Bangkok in April 1982.

Enter a python: Thailand – 1982-89

With my journey to Thailand, my life became an overseas mission that has never stopped. I lived in a typical house on stilts in Aranyaprathet village, where access to most of the camps was reasonable along red laterite roads, except for dodging tanks and occasional bullets. (The only bullets I didn't manage to dodge lodged miraculously in the cheap metal door of our pick-up truck.) In the deep mud of the rainy season, however, a blind elephant was the only viable transport to Refugee Camp Site 8.

Thousands of Cambodians were fleeing west into Thailand from the megalomaniac Pol Pot's regime, which ultimately caused the deaths of approximately three million Khmers and decimated the country's rich cultural heritage. My initial six-month commitment stretched to eight years. Bombs flew as the rebel resistance factions running the camps fought the invaders of their beloved country, which the new regime had named Kampuchea. The United Nations and dozens of non-governmental organisations (NGOs) literally picked up the pieces, providing food, water, medication, education and countless prostheses. Thousands waited desperately for a pass for 'the Third Country' – any new country of refuge far from the genocide – having escaped country one, Cambodia, for temporary exile in a camp in country two, Thailand. When we bid each other farewell, we would say, 'Meet you in *Proté ti Bowen*' – country four: heaven.

During this time, Tiglath Pileser the Squeezer, my four-metre python who was rescued from becoming multiple steaks, came and went, eventually being released ceremoniously into a national park. I also swam with the water buffalo at the end of the long, hot, emotional days. I was relieved to be told by survivors of the genocide that *God was indeed there*. Khao-i-Dang bamboo church became home to the largest Cambodian congregation in the world, filled with extraordinary stories of miraculous escapes, tigers instead of ravens providing food for the starving, and octogenarians learning to read the Bible because of their newfound faith.

One morning a boy huddled at the back of the church, with criss-cross bamboo shadows on his face. Perhaps twelve years old, little Sato had survived an illegal night incursion into the camp, but his friend had died in the attempt. Now the church elders wanted me to adopt him. He couldn't return home to Battambang across a mined war zone, nor could he stay in Khao-i-Dang. To placate the elders and salve my conscience, I applied for asylum on his behalf, confident the British government would refuse my request because they only accepted Vietnamese orphans. An exception was made: Sato was accepted. The British organisation that received him saw no anomaly in placing a Cambodian child in an orphanage full of Vietnamese, although the two countries were at war with each other. Sato suffered indelibly in the institution but eventually emerged a young adult and married a wonderful Cambodian. With their two children, they earned a living in London cooking Cambodian, Thai and Vietnamese food.

Samaki spies: Cambodia – 1989-94

Eight years in Aranyaprathet with Christian Outreach seemed enough. By 1989 I was fluent in Khmer and could no longer resist the call to Cambodia. The country was still occupied by Vietnam, who boasted of having liberated it from the demonic clutches of the Khmer Rouge. Teaching English seemed the only way to get a visa so I duly did a crash course in London and was accepted by the World Council of Churches as an English teacher in Phnom Penh. There, in the ruined Samaki Hotel, bats controlled the third floor, monkeys ran the second floor and on the first floor non-communist expatriates enjoyed the former glory of the old colonial hotel. It was important to hide your Bible and to be very circumspect about all Christian activities – the communist regime was rabidly anti-Christian. A $10 bicycle helped me throw off my government-appointed spy and spend weekends with my adopted Khmer Christian family in Tumnop Tuk village out of town.

Here I received my education about how many impoverished Cambodians were living: eating boiled red ants and other unmentionables; coiling the innards of burst tyres to sell in the market; sleeping on the floor, of course; and attending joyful illegal church on Sunday. Exactly a decade before, I had experienced the same thrill worshipping in the underground church in Russia, with faith and risk holding hands for a divine encounter.

In 1990, hotly wedged in a long winding snake of ancient rusty Russian tanks, the Vietnamese pulled out of Cambodia. Cynics said, 'Watch the cats. If the cat population decreases, they have really left.' (The Vietnamese were very partial to eating cats.) 'Otherwise, they are simply filtering back in through porous borders to continue their communist subversion.' By candlelight we read the new government edict announcing freedom of worship, but literally by daybreak the united underground church had split into factions. United under oppression, sadly liberty brought the pain of division. As well as promoting creative evangelism and interpreting, one of my early jobs with World Vision was trying to build cohesion among the various Christian groups.

In August 1994 I was still in Phnom Penh when news of an African genocide between two ethnic groups provoked a prayer dialogue between me and God: 'Go to Rwanda.' 'But I'm scared of dead bodies.' 'Perfect love casts out fear.' 'But I don't have perfect love.' 'Jesus is perfect love and you have me.' 'Oh, okay then.' World Vision sent me to Rwanda to gather up lost children and run a temporary orphanage. My qualifications: I spoke French and appeared to be able to function in places with zero security. I flew with a contract that was initially for only three months.

The belly of the whale: Rwanda – 1994-97

Rwanda then was a land of brave orphans, of anguish and impossible questions. A land of heaped bodies. A land still loved by God, although some wondered whether he had fallen asleep.

One September night I was driving south from the capital Kigali to my home in Gikongoro. This was in the French Zone Turquoise, established as a security perimeter but by then abandoned by almost all expatriates. Rain and earth-warmth created the illusion of hundreds of tall, wispy ghosts crowding the road while on and on and on I drove crying – crying bitter tears as God showed me how many had died in the Rwandan genocide. Yet early the next sunny morning, my magnificent chicken Kibuye woke me as usual by pecking on the door of my home – a green tent – until I unzipped it to deliver her breakfast of rice grain, gently eaten from my palm. Consolation comes in many forms.

Tracing and placing children separated from family during the chaotic genocide was an emotional task. Relatives were traumatised, the country destabilised, with nationwide killing heaping poverty on top of pre-existing poverty. Some relatives were impossible to find, some confirmed dead and some unenthusiastic to open doors to any but immediate family. However, the tears of successful reunions almost made up for the failures.

The time came when our World Vision Gikongoro Centre needed to be closed and two girls remained: Ketya, the child of witch doctors, and Alexa, with osteomyelitis (a serious bone infection). At last, in response to my shameless emotional blackmail, a European couple in the lakeside village of Kibogora agreed to take our little Alexa, and couldn't refuse when in desperation I thrust Ketya on them also.

Soon after, all the villages around began to receive death threats from the Hutu rebels, and one by one the attacks were carried out as advertised. Next on the hit list, Kibogora received its own midnight warning, and a group of us gathered in the living room to pray as we had never prayed before. We were in the belly of the whale; in the heart of God. We had nowhere to run, knowing we would die; we knew we couldn't die. We were strangely praying in liquid joy, praying in peace that passed all understanding, praying in the power of perfect unity. It was terrible and exquisite. I have never been so acutely vulnerable and so divinely blessed.

We heard our attackers approaching, we saw their fire, but no one came. No one. As we had rejoiced all night, we rejoiced in the morning. Humbled and amazed, I drove home alone across the forest, back to Gikongoro.

Putrid wild boar: back to Cambodia – 1997-98

By 1997 life began to stabilise and I knew it was time to cut ties. World Concern offered me a dream job for six months in an isolated village in Prey Veng province, back in Cambodia. My mandate was to evangelise the village of Preah Sdach. Here I learnt to collect water using a treadle pump, learnt to eat dog meat with the village chief (I couldn't refuse) and watched the Holy Spirit come in power. And here, during a coup d'état, I learnt not to be afraid until you really need to be afraid – a useful lesson for the rest of my life.

My happy six months ended in a visit to a tribal village in the north, where I unwisely accepted a meal of potent home brew and putrid wild boar from a tribal chief (again, I couldn't refuse). Flying back to Phnom Penh (when, incidentally, I was also asked to transport a box containing the head of a rabid dog for testing), I was soon feverish, then in and out of consciousness and hospitals until a wheelchair exit from Bangkok brought me home to family in the UK. Finally a meningeal virus was diagnosed. As I slowly regained strength, a call came from World Vision Burundi: 'Where are you? We have tens of thousands of orphans in the hills and we need you!'

Taming war obstacles: Burundi – 1998-2020

I arrived in war-torn Burundi in 1998, where a one-year commitment stretched to twenty-two years. One of the verses that was special to me at this time was Psalm 34:18: 'The LORD is close to the broken-hearted and saves those who are crushed in spirit.' I was living in Gitega, in the centre of Burundi, in the rebel supply corridor between Tanzania and north-west Burundi. My job, together with my team in four provinces, was to support war orphans in child-headed households (families headed by the eldest child because their parents were dead). Rebel activity was constant in the forests around us. It was also here that the visiting evangelist Bahati from Rwanda prophetically baptised me 'Mbabazi', meaning 'Compassion'.

One day, with the team on our way to Gishubi commune in the Land Cruiser, we were surrounded by rebels. It was bound to happen sooner or later. 'We need your car!' 'Well, you're not having my car. I need my car – and anyway it isn't mine to give.' My last, unspoken argument was, *'Besides, I don't even know if you are the good guys or the bad guys.'* Not expecting resistance, especially from a white female, they didn't know how to break me. Eventually we heard cries and the approach of running footsteps in the trees, whereupon, in disgust, they abandoned negotiations and fled. We drove off before the other good/bad guys could appear.

In Kayanza we regularly ate at Chez le Lion on the main street. It seemed to defy gravity on its rickety wooden stilts, but definitely served the best, cheapest meal in town. It also fortified us for all the unpredictability of the security situation – with home visits to isolated orphans and rebel messages on the blackboards of wrecked schools reminding us that Big Brother was watching.

After each meal at Chez le Lion, a boy would be waiting outside – a slight, hooded figure, with his badly damaged hand pulling the hood across a face I didn't dare to imagine. For too many weeks, in my cowardice, I thrust money in his claw hand so he would just go away, as if trying to reduce him to not being. I was trying to ignore my screaming conscience, begging, 'Stop it! I can't help everyone in the world, can I?'

Eventually I dared to know Freddy, to talk to him, to decipher the words that came from the gaping hole that was once a mouth – seven years previously, aged seven, he'd fallen into a fire while having an epileptic fit and broken open his jaw. God taught me to look him in his torn eyes and accord him the value of a human being – a challenge to my lifelong issue with my own unbeauty. And I ended up buying him a new face in Kigali. I think it took fifteen surgeries, with kind friends contributing to accumulating costs. Today he has a face, a faith, a medical degree, a wife and two beautiful children. 'One starfish at a time', the story goes: even if we can only take one small step to relieve suffering, it's better than nothing.

After ten years of financial security at World Vision, I was invited to join a new local Burundian organisation in 1998. I was attracted by the risk, by its small size and by the simplicity of its mission: to evangelise and serve the poor. This organisation was based in the capital, Bujumbura. Near my office was the central prison, Mpimba, where I was a frequent visitor. To get there I walked past cotton and bean fields where green-clad prisoners were working. The building had space and plumbing designed for 3,000 but housed at least 5,000 inmates. The menu was calculated to just keep a person alive, but conditions were such that at one point there were multiple deaths weekly. Here I was also introduced to the heartless spectre of death row. I confess I was the first person to smuggle a mobile phone into the prison, where it fit neatly into a flask, after Mr P said he needed one 'for emergencies'. And the emergency came: 'Where are you? I need you to bring charcoal to cook rice – we are starving.'

As it happened, the capital was under siege at the time, with the prison situated in the epicentre of the violence. So I protested I would have to risk my life to deliver charcoal. 'Just bring it!' I was told. I bought the charcoal, at an elevated price of course, ran the gauntlet of rebel artillery in the Musaga quarter past our office, and received a hero's welcome when I arrived safely, heart pounding, at the gates of Mpimba, where security measures were waived. Ironically, I felt safer there in prison than anywhere else, and put off for as long as possible the drive home. Once I had persuaded myself to leave, I drove home unscathed, my heart still pounding.

Some months later, while working with demobilised child soldiers, one of our teenage girl trainees told me she had been there that very day, her machine gun mounted on a tripod on the hill and shooting at the time I was driving through. The notorious group who had conscripted her always preferred to put children in the front lines.

Still concerned for Mr P, on death row, I mobilised my small nieces and nephews to pray for him. Eventually he was miraculously released by a presidential pardon. Having converted in prison, he married, became a lawyer and today frequently evangelises on radio and beyond.

Yes, there were many tense moments, but God always opens the door to joy. With Liz, my housemate and school principal, I was relaxing one day by Lake Tanganyika as the sun began dripping down the Mulenge mountains across the lake in the Congo. To our great delight a hippo who frequented our lake shore waddled into the shallows, before suddenly reversing his substantial posterior into a nearby bush. Very nearby. I started filming before we realised what was happening. A territorial ritual was in full swing, with his funny little tail spinning like a fan and poo flying everywhere. We covered our drinks, choking with hysteria. For weeks to come, if ever we needed cheering up, the priceless video was produced.

Part of our work involved inviting girls off the streets to learn sewing. Most of these girls were lowest-income operators, paid extra for services without a condom. Sofia's clients were upper-class. She quickly showed technical aptitude in her sewing but was cold to the praise, prayer and teaching that preceded each day's lessons. Then we began to notice that her clothes were becoming more modest, the make-up was less lurid and her spirit was softening. One day she asked if she could spend the weekend at the office on a prayer retreat, in preparation for a visit to her family. That weekend she symbolically burned the clothes of her previous trade and consolidated a relationship with the God who had planned all along to hold her in his arms and show her the love she had sought elsewhere for too long.

Sofia's family had rejected her when they found out she was living a life of prostitution, but she wanted to go back to her village to ask for forgiveness and share her newfound faith. We granted her a few days off and prayed as she set off home up the steep, familiar mountain tracks. As she neared her village, she heard sounds of a party reverberating around the hills. The previous day God had revealed to her brother that they were to buy a goat and prepare a celebration for a special visitor that God would bring. Obedient to the revelation, the party was made ready. When Sofia arrived, nervous about her reception, it was to her own feast. She also found out that many had come to faith since she left and there was even a church in the village. All night long stories of God's faithfulness amazed and thrilled both family and community: the prodigal had been restored.

I was entering my twenty-second year in Burundi and feeling the Lord hinting at new vistas when the unthinkable happened: Sato's beautiful five-year-old daughter, Allison Blair, contracted inoperable brain cancer. She eventually flew with her distraught mother from England to Battambang, Cambodia to bid farewell to her grandparents. In a memorable poolside conversation in Bujumbura, I was persuaded by a British stranger, God's emissary, to pack a small bag and fly from Burundi to Cambodia for ten days to add my farewells. At the same time the emissary, Jon Bicknell, suggested I investigate the situation regarding Bible translations into the minority languages of north-east Cambodia. Days after landing, covid restrictions were put in place and all airports and provincial borders were closed. I never saw Allison again but, from my exile in Banlung in the Ratanakiri province, was able to speak to her almost daily to the moment of her death. In his infinite wisdom God used my brave little namesake to take me across the world from my Burundi home to a new vocation in north-eastern Cambodia.

Baby dragons and Bible translation: north-eastern Cambodia – 2020-24

The Kavet people are one of the last minorities in Cambodia to begin a Bible translation, coinciding with my arrival in 2020 under the auspices of YWAM and led by my old friend Philip Scott from the Thai border refugee camps in the 1980s. Dabbling with runes and hieroglyphics as a small child, making my way through the Cyrillic alphabet in school then moving from the longest alphabet in the world (Khmer) to, purportedly, the most complex grammatical structure in existence (Kinyarwanda/Kirundi), Kavet was an obvious next step for me.

By the time airports and borders began to open tentatively in the unpredictable, covid-shredded world, I knew I would return to Cambodia and Kavetland after a last visit to Burundi. I bid farewell to my one-eyed kitten, Princess Nefertiti, who faithfully sat on my shoulder throughout my exile stresses. There was no doubt that God was calling me to 'enlarge the place of your tent, stretch your tent curtains wide' (Isaiah 54:2), but that didn't soften the blow of leaving Burundi after twenty-two years. To paraphrase C.S. Lewis, if you don't want your heart to break, wrap it up carefully and lock it away in a box – but when you return to it, you will find it has turned to stone. World Vision's Bob Pierce asked God to break his heart with the things that break the heart of God. We can choose.

Then came the verse calling me to work with the Kavet people: 'I am sending you … to open their eyes and turn them from darkness to light, and from the power of Satan to God, so that they may receive forgiveness of sins and a place among those who are sanctified by faith in me' (Acts 26:17–18). And so, last (so far) but not least, my journey ends in the Land of Baby Dragons – *draco volans*, if you don't believe me. Fly into the capital of Buddhist Cambodia, drive north for nine, ten or eleven hours – depending on how deep the mud is – and there on the Sekong River you will find my new home: Siem Pang. It is defined north and south by large spirit houses for the particularly ugly gods of water and land but also by the beautiful wooden bridges often swarmed by monkeys, of which a few are disconcertingly aggressive. The length of the High Street you can also find cows, lumbering water buffaloes, Vietnamese pot-bellied pigs and territorial dogs. And rather small children riding too-large motorbikes. Here everyone feels safe – as long as you don't happen by chance to witness a night delivery of heroin from upriver, for example. Or speak up about corruption, or endangered animals and widespread illegal logging of the rainforest. Or have an altercation with cow horns, scorpions in the sink or a Chinese red-headed centipede. Or…

If you then take the raft ferry across the river at Koh Chan, you are in Kavetland. It is another world. Another language. You may find a village sacrificing a water buffalo to the spirits for the ritual healing of a sick or possessed resident. You may find another village praising God in the Kavet language in a wooden house on stilts. Ubiquitous dogs may be under foot or on your dinner plate. The Kavet myth of creation is that they were issue of a woman and a dog. Allegedly the same dog, growing hungry afloat during a flood, ate the piece of buffalo hide on which was written the Kavet alphabet – hence their humiliating illiteracy until recently.

YWAM oversees a twenty-year-old evening Kavet Literacy Programme, whose teachers are all Kavet volunteers, most of whom learnt to read and write in evening classes. Bunthan learnt to read aged fourteen. Today he is not only head of the Literacy Programme but also a key translator of the New Testament, which is already at the revision stage pre-publication. When we both have time, I sit beside his Khmer–Kavet split screen as he types, waving my Greek–English Interlinear New Testament and pretending I am part of the process. Kavet songs, short Bible stories and village-based training in Oral Bible-Storytelling for the illiterate (whereby I memorise the stories by heart and then villagers learn them by repetition and drama) all nurture the Kavet understanding of who they are in God's unfolding plan. Graciously accepting me into their community, they are helping me also to appreciate who I am in God's formidable unfolding plan, anointed with the oil of joy.

NB Some names have been changed to protect identities.

5

DAVID CAMPBELL

JAMAICA

Trench Town, Jamaica – 1999

'So dis is the Englishman I have been speaking with on the phone! Beloved, it is great to meet you!'

'It is good to meet you too, Bobby!'

'Well, let's take you to Trench Town!'

After this greeting, Bobby beckoned me to the passenger seat of his white sedan, a Russian-made Lada. We set off, weaving through the back roads to avoid Kingston's traffic. I was twenty-two. My fourth stay in Jamaica. My first meeting with Pastor Bobby Wilmot.

He was in his early forties at the time, a man of relatively dark complexion and an almost permanent grin that revealed his brilliant-white teeth. He had a small pendant around his neck with the words 'Destined to Win' painted on it, and a belt with three mobile phones arranged on his sides like pistols in an old Western cowboy film.

As he drove, Bobby explained the downward spiral of poverty, politics, the cocaine trade and the gang leaders, known as Dons, which had all been factors in creating the challenges that Trench Town faced. When gang violence had spiralled out of control during the eighties and early nineties, people who could afford to get out, got out. Businesses and schools closed down. Trench Town became poorer than ever. As Bobby drove from our meeting spot in 'uptown' Kingston into 'downtown' Kingston, the streets became less maintained, the buildings older, the houses less tidy.

Bobby was overflowing with enthusiasm and hope as he told me how, after two decades of this downward spiral, a small group of Christians had walked right into the heart of Trench Town in 1988, carrying a nine-foot wooden cross. They stopped on the borderline that marked the political divide and prayed for restoration. That time of prayer was a defining moment for Pastor Bobby in his calling, and from then on he would repeatedly declare that the community belonged to Jesus. He believed that it would be known as a place of joy, and stayed with a handful of others to play their part in the vision of a transformed community.

He parked his Lada outside a school compound, and we went in to meet his wife, Jenny, and see the school they had started together, named Joy Town. Jenny was warm and welcoming, and clearly very dedicated to the children. We then went to meet Lorna Stanley at the Operation Restoration building. When Bobby had told her about the need for education in Trench Town, she had given up a career in PR in Miami to return to Jamaica and start a remedial high school in Trench Town. I was impressed by her love for the young people, and her passionate commitment to the community.

Bobby then took me on a walk around the community, and I was struck by the number of people along the streets who 'hailed him up' (greeted him). We walked down into the section known as Rema, and Bobby pointed to the end of the road as the major political borderline, right between Rema and Denham Town. There were derelict buildings which had once been a school and several empty houses, overgrown with weeds, where the residents had left because of the violence and never returned. Someone who knew Bobby approached him to ask about something, so I took a few steps further around the corner to get a better look at the open plot of land. To me, it just looked like a potential open space where we could build a basketball court, which was what I was there for. As I began to walk out towards the land, I felt a small hand clasp tightly onto mine and tug me back towards the street corner. I turned around to see a young boy who was around seven or eight years old, his eyes alert with fear and concern.

'Don't go out there, sir … dem 'ave an open shot.'

He kept tugging my hand, so I went back behind the protection of the wall at the corner, still only beginning to comprehend that this young child was fearing for my life. There were certain lines that you couldn't cross, dangerous places to walk in the open and everyone – even the children – knew how things ran. Having spent my childhood between a farm in West Dorset and British boarding school, I was now in a completely different context and had a lot to learn.

To that child, Bobby's dream of the community being a place of joy may have felt like an impossible dream.

No individual person or group, other than Christ himself, can say that they orchestrated all that happened in the coming years … but impossible things happened. Before going further into the story, I had better explain how I got to Jamaica in the first place.

Running away from school – 1994

My palms felt clammy, my heart raced and my stomach was churning as I stood in front of the counter, looking at the chubby face and greying hair of the post office worker. He had asked a simple question: 'Would you like that as a cheque, or in cash?' I was seventeen, and trying hard to look as though this experience was completely in my stride.

'Er, I'll just take the cash please.'

He paused for what may have only been a few seconds … but I can remember looking into those eyes. The dark frames of his glasses intensified his gaze and a tingling feeling surged up from my toes. I was so afraid that he would tell someone what I was up to … but his next words were in a cheerful tone: 'Well let's get you a bag then!'

I had been planning to buy a car when I was eighteen, so had been saving any money I was given for birthday presents, my inheritance from my grandfathers and anything I earned from summer jobs. I had then abandoned that original plan in the year leading up to this moment because I had realised there was something else I needed far more.

Some crazy experiences with a Ouija board at boarding school had convinced me there is a very real spiritual realm. Reading some of the Gospel of Mark had convinced me that Jesus was a completely unique character who was worth listening to. A medical missionary to Afghanistan who spoke at school had convinced me that what I needed most of all was Jesus, and to know his mission for my life.

So I was closing the account, not to buy a car, but to buy a ticket to Jamaica. I have been asked 'Why Jamaica?' more times than I can remember, and the only answer I have ever had is that I just had a strange sense that was the right place to go.

There were no flights to Jamaica from Heathrow that day, but I got a ticket to fly from Gatwick the following day. This meant I had to spend the night in the airport. I kept wondering if school would tell the police and if they would find me before I got away. I did manage to find the airport chapel, a simple room with a few chairs, Bibles, a table with a cloth and a large cross on the wall. It was a quiet oasis in a bustling place – a perfect place to pause, reflect that this was really happening and have a try at talking to God. I got on my knees and awkwardly wondered how to start. One thing that the medical missionary had said was that if you gave your life to God and asked him to live in your heart, he would. That was the whole reason for this crazy move, so I thought I had better ask him to do that now.

'Er … hey God … um … I don't even know if you are real … but I kind of really hope you are right now. … Er … I'm making this step because I just don't want to keep living my own way, and I don't want to keep living the way other people tell me I should … I want to live the way you say. So … yeah … my life is yours now … to keep … um … and if that's okay with you, can you come now … and live in me? … Yep … er … thanks.'

Though the words were clumsy, my heart was sincere, and for the first time in my life I experienced the most profound sense of peace, rightness and closeness with God. I don't know for exactly how long, but I just knelt there in silence with my eyes closed for some time, enjoying the presence of the one I had been yearning for.

The next day I arrived in Jamaica, and it wasn't long before I realised that God had answered my need for him, as well as my need to know his mission for my life.

Trench Town, Jamaica – 2002

After working with Pastor Bobby in 1999 and 2000, I crossed America with my two sisters on a three-person bicycle in 2001 to raise money for a community centre. I then moved to Jamaica in 2002. By then Bobby was working closely with another pastor, Errol Henry, to help churches work together and reach out to the community. We organised a forty-day season of prayer and fasting, with different people across the churches signing up to fast and pray on the different days.

Pastor Bobby and an elder from his church, Major Cooke, had started a charity: the Joy Town Community Development Foundation. One of their goals was to promote interaction and peace in the community through sport. I was given the task of organising a football 'Peace Competition', with teams from sixteen communities. The challenge was that all these communities had a history of violence against one another.

When one player scored two goals, meaning his team won, the supporters of the losing team were angry. According to them he was over age for the competition. The shouting and threats began to get very heated, and then a warning shot was fired into the air. Almost immediately the other side fired another shot. This was to say to one another, 'If you want to start, we're ready.'

We managed to get the supporters to disperse, but the team coaches then came to me, still angry about the injustice in the competition. Many of the registration forms from all the teams turned out to have false information, so there was no solid ground to resolve the dispute fairly. I had agreed to run this league to bring peace, but it was threatening to cause serious conflict.

The forty-day season of fasting concluded that same day, with a prayer march including all the different churches. As we came to one of the 'corners' where the bloodshed has been at its worst over the years, people were kneeling on the ground and praying for cleansing, and for God to change the spiritual atmosphere in the area.

A few days later I met with all the coaches of the football teams, and something had mysteriously changed. I was intending to cancel the competition, but when I tried to say that, they didn't seem to hear. Instead, they negotiated peacefully and respectfully about what had gone wrong and how to sort it out. So the remaining matches went ahead, with a completely different spirit. The losers accepted defeat graciously, the winners did not gloat, the supporters even complimented and encouraged the referees for being fair.

The final was between the same two sides that had almost gone to war, and the match went through full time, extra time and a golden goal to a penalty shoot-out, which was won 6-5! A huge crowd from the neighbourhood had turned out for the nail-biting final, following which they all came into the Ambassador Theatre in the middle of Trench Town for the trophy presentation. It was the first time that people from all these rival corners had come together like that peacefully. The sense of unity was so strong that they cheered and clapped for each other's successes – it was so different to what had been happening earlier in the competition.

Another transformation happened within days, but started brutally. Gang members from Rema went and threw bottles with petrol and flaming rags into nine houses in the rival community of Denham Town, setting them ablaze. Revenge came a few nights later, when gunmen from Denham Town crept into Rema and kicked in the door of a house, spraying shots inside. The victims were a sixteen-year-old girl who was pregnant, and a three-year-old child. After investing so much in working and praying for change, the other church leaders and I were just devastated by this.

When someone in the gangs is killed, the community members can get angry, but there is a general acceptance that if you live by the gun, you are likely to die by the gun. However, when innocent girls and children are killed, the community is so hurt that it looks to its men to carry out a revenge attack. The pressure on these guys in Rema to take vengeance was incredibly strong … but something had changed since that time of prayer.

After a series of meetings with Bobby, Lorna Stanley (of Operation Restoration), myself, the man who was leading the most influential gang in Rema at the time, and a Rastaman they respected, the gang leaders made a commitment that there would be no reprisal. Wanted men do not like to be on camera, so they asked Lorna to go on the news to announce this. She was able to assure the other community that she had spoken to the men from Rema and there would be no more killing.

The cycle of violence was interrupted that day, which was a significant step between these communities. The conflict had been raging for thirty years, so Bobby and the other church leaders who had been praying for this were overjoyed to see change start.

Greece, Australia and fresh ideas – 2003-04

In October 2003, at the invitation of a Jamaican pastor, I attended a sports ministry conference in Athens. Afterwards, when I was standing in the check-in line of Athens airport, I met an Aussie called Marty Woods. He recognised me as 'the white guy' who had stood up with all the delegates from the Caribbean at the conference. Marty was part of an Australian mission organisation called Fusion, who had a long history of bringing people together with a spirit of celebration and co-operation, instead of with activities that promote competition. I was fascinated to learn of Fusion's approach, even more so because another 'Peace Competition' in Trench Town in 2003 had led to another incident where warning shots were fired between rival gangs. While God intervened again, the repeated pattern meant that I was searching for different ways to bring people together in the community.

By early 2004 I had my first opportunity to attend some of Fusion's training in Australia. It was inspiring and refreshing to meet a large community of people who were deeply committed to Jesus and to finding ways to make a difference in the lives of young people in their community.

One of the things that I had overlooked as a zealous missionary, from a highly individualistic culture, was that it takes a community to reach a community. I had been sharing the gospel through basketball clubs and seeing young people come to faith, but had not been forming communities who shared a mission focus within the wider community. Where community events had been happening, it was much more through me powering ahead on my own. I hadn't worked out how to slow down and involve the young people from the community itself. The Fusion approach changed that, as it was very relational and helped us connect with young people at different stages on their spiritual journey.

We held the first Fusion event in December 2004, learnt on the job and adapted the model to be effective in Jamaica's inner-city culture. Two years later Liz, who I had met in Australia and then married, came to join me in Jamaica to develop the work there. A local team began to grow, and we put all the elements of Fusion's approach to mission in place. We started working in the local schools to give a chaplaincy presence for the students. We started after-school clubs for youth, and then for children as well. We started running a youth café so young people would have a safe place to hang out. We started taking young people on outward-bound trips to waterfalls, beaches and gardens where they would have an amazing day out, and then hear a testimony and a gospel presentation. We started a youth Bible study for those who became Christians. Hundreds of young people gave their lives to Christ through this approach, and a community of young people grew who were equipped for serving in mission through the exciting, fun and positive community events. Alongside the positive impact on individuals, we literally saw – many times – community wars turn to peace when their young people served together through these events.

Being sent to church as a child is normal for a lot of Jamaicans, but many do not continue going as adults. Jamar was one young person who had grown up in church. After joining the basketball club, coming on trips, joining the Bible Study and serving at community events, he said:

> I have been going to church here in Trench Town my whole life, and I don't know how many times I have heard people praying for the violence to stop. To be honest I didn't think God would ever answer that prayer … but now I see the prayers being answered. What I never expected was that he would use me as part of the answer.

Another young person was George, also known as Shaboo. He left school without completing any subjects, his older brother was a gang member who was shot and killed, his father was not around in the home, and he had a tough relationship with his mother. When Shaboo started coming on the trips, he was spending his days begging at the traffic lights and his nights dancing at the dancehalls in the street; he had no hope for his future. He gave his life to the Lord at a summer camp, and one of the Fusion team, Robert Dixon, began to mentor him. We got him back into school at Youth Reaching Youth, and through this school he met Crystal. Today they are married with two children and Shaboo is a loving and present father, as well as being one of the leaders of Fusion Jamaica.

His testimony is one of complete transformation, and his ministry continues to impact the next generation of young people growing up in similar circumstances.

God can save your life? – 2008

It was getting close to 11 p.m. but I had just dropped home the last team member who had attended training that evening. We always used our ministry bus to get people home safely, especially if it was late. As I turned the corner at Majesty Gardens to head home, a man stepped out, holding a semi-automatic gun with an extended clip, which he waved to show me that he wanted me to stop. He came over to my open window and asked me for money to buy food. Another man emerged from beside a rusty sheet-metal fence behind him, and then another from the other side of the road. As the conversation with the first man went back and forth, he was posturing with his chest high, saying, 'We run the place yu know.'

God's Spirit comes alive in you in certain moments, and this was one of those. I was overwhelmed with love for this broken and lost young man. Somehow I could just calmly say to him, 'Actually, God runs the place.' I could see the confusion and the spiritual struggle within him.

Those spirits took over and his face contorted menacingly, his head nodded back as he threateningly asked, 'God can save your life?'

Again, all I could see was someone in desperate need of the truth. So I looked him straight in the eye, deep into his soul, and said, 'Yes. Yes he can.'

In that exact moment headlights appeared as another car turned onto the road and started driving towards us, lighting up the darkness where the three men were standing around my bus. The gunman seemed confused, not sure who to focus on, and his friends grew visibly agitated.

'Squeeze it now, man! Squeeze it!' said the second man, encouraging the gunman to squeeze the trigger. But he took a step back from my window and raised his weapon towards the oncoming car, confused by the lights – and the amount of weed he'd been smoking.

I saw the opportunity to move, so calmly put the engine into gear and drove off slowly past the oncoming car. I knew I was still an easy target until I reached the corner, so I prayed all the way, but still felt completely calm … until I was around the corner and on the main road, when I began to shake all over.

The following day a local pastor who knew many of the gang members invited me to come back to Majesty Gardens and meet with all of the gang. He got the main leader to tell them all not to touch me because I was doing good things for the youth in the community, and then I got to speak to all the young men. I shared with them that I was not afraid for myself because I knew where I was going – heaven. But I said that I was afraid for them because of the choices they were making with their lives, and encouraged them all to turn to Christ. Some of them were too hardened to hear, including the gunman who sadly was killed only two months later, but others were listening deeply. So what started as a threatening incident became a great opportunity to speak into some young men's lives.

Reconciliation – 2010

By 2010 the team in Jamaica had run over 100 community events across Trench Town and other inner-city communities … which turned out to be crucial preparation for a key moment.

Kingston is a noisy city. There is constant traffic; frequent blaring of car horns; loud revving of the two-stroke engines of Yeng Yeng bikes; music playing from many directions at once; a lot of people on the streets; and helicopters occasionally passing by overhead. That all went eerily silent in May 2010.

Jamaica's most notorious don, a man known as Dudus, was a major player in the drug trade as well as being behind multiple murders. The US wanted to extradite him, but when the Jamaican government agreed, he saw this as a personal 'dis' (an act of disrespect). He gathered criminals from across Jamaica to come and join him in Tivoli Gardens, and they attacked police stations and prepared the community for a siege. We were glued to the news as the drama unfolded, and were constantly calling and messaging team members, checking if they were safe.

A national state of emergency was declared and all residents were required to stay at home while the government scrambled to respond. We lived in the middle of Kingston at the time, and had never heard it so quiet.

When the dust settled, the army had taken control of Tivoli Gardens, Dudus had fled through a tunnel, and seventy-three people in Tivoli Gardens had been killed. One of them was a young man, Roofy, who we had mentored through the basketball programme and Fusion's other youth activities, which had been running for eight years by then. He had gone to visit his mother in Tivoli Gardens, but could not leave when the siege happened, which ended up costing him his life. While Dudus eventually turned himself in, it was a very confronting and sad time for Jamaica. For the children in Tivoli Gardens, it was traumatic.

The Umbrella Group of Churches was looking for ways to respond, and Fusion Jamaica was given the task of running some community-building activities for the children. We ran a series of community festivals over the following year, with each set of festivals running over three consecutive days, to give the children and young people an opportunity to come together through play. We didn't even know how effective this would be until years later, when a child psychologist from Canada called Dr Jeanne Williams started partnering with us and teaching us the impact of play for healing post trauma. Yet God obviously knew and used those festivals not only for the children, but also to bring together people and churches from both sides of the borderline as one team.

That December, children from schools across Tivoli Gardens and Denham Town marched through the streets in costume to celebrate the Christmas story. We had started this celebration in Trench Town a couple of years before, having got the idea from Fusion in Australia. The children were dressed as angels, wise men and shepherds, with Joseph and Mary leading the way. We had arranged for different business places and the police station to be the innkeepers that Joseph would approach to ask if there was any room for his wife to have her baby. When each replied that there was 'no room at the inn', the procession would move on until finally space was found in a stable.

And so a massive crowd of children, teachers, parents and community members, all in Christmas costumes, surrounded Denham Town Police Station that year. It was a powerful moment of reconciliation between the police and the community, because it was one of the stations that had been set on fire.

The following Christmas, twelve and a half years after that little boy warned me not to walk out where I might get shot, I was standing in the middle of the same plot of land. This time there were hundreds of children from all over Trench Town, Denham Town and Tivoli Gardens playing together. Children from schools on both sides of the borderline had marched in Christmas costumes, in two large processions, to come together on that plot of land and act out the Christmas story.

After the story finished with the Prince of Peace being born, we ran a series of games and activities. The last of these was a 'tug-of-peace' (because we don't do 'tug-of-war' in these communities). It was girls against boys, and the best of three. After the girls won the first round, the boys came back to win the second. Everything rested on the last round. The girls recruited every lady they could see anywhere nearby … and won. Cheers, dancing, smiles and laughter filled the area, and I couldn't help remembering two things: that young boy who grabbed my hand when I first set foot on that plot of land, and Pastor Bobby's vision for reconciliation and a community marked by joy.

New life – 2018

In 2018, though, we realised that the community mission focus had subtly overtaken our focus on making disciples. As a leader, I had started to care more about people turning up to help run programmes than I did about them and their walk with Christ. Change was needed. So we started a fellowship group on Sunday afternoons where people first met in groups of three, did a discovery Bible study together and then shared a meal. For all who came, this put their relationship with Christ right back at the centre of how we did things … and suddenly God started turning up in the mission work in new ways. People were growing spiritually, lives were being changed, healings started happening and miracles of provision continued – all in God's timing.

Even when covid happened, we were able to give away four times our monthly budget every month in the form of food packages and prayer outreaches. The Jamaican team became strong enough for Liz and I to hand the leadership over to them in August 2022. We continue to support the team and are now focused on releasing more workers for similar ministry. Meanwhile the work of peacemaking has continued in the community, and Fusion Jamaica now runs a centre in a building right on the borderline.

Pastor Bobby went to be with the Lord in 2020, but not before seeing a lot of answers to his prayers for Trench Town. The school building on the borderline that had been derelict in 1999 was restored and has been running again for years. Families moved into the area and rebuilt the homes, and new housing developments were built. The murder rate dropped, hundreds of young people gave their lives to Christ and educational achievement in the community went up.

6

DIEUDONNE NAHIMANA

BURUNDI

Muyinga, Burundi – 1982

It was still dark as I set out for school in my khaki uniform. My feet were bare running through the bush and I carried a lunch of beans and plantain wrapped in a banana leaf. Although I had shoes, they had to be kept for church, even on cold mornings like today. I was nearly nine years old, and the youngest of eight siblings. My older brothers and sisters had already moved away to schools in different areas.

I knew it was an honour for me to go to primary school, and it was where I would learn to speak French, but it was a twelve-kilometre journey through the bush to get to lessons. I had to leave home at 6 a.m. to arrive for the start of school at 7.30 a.m.

I'm from the north-east part of Burundi, the region of Muyinga, west of the Tanzanian border and south of Rwanda. My father told me that before colonialism, Rwanda and Burundi were two separate kingdoms with different kings. The Germans colonised both countries in the 1890s. Then in 1916, after the defeat of German forces during the First World War, Belgium took over control, later governing them as the combined territory of Ruanda-Urundi. But in 1962, Rwanda and Burundi gained independence as two separate states.

I was often scared in the bush as I made my way to school, wary of snakes or the processionary caterpillars that in certain seasons came down from the trees and could cause boils, hives and severe pain if they fell on you.

In the rainy season, as I walked to school, I would get soaked. I felt as if I had a constant cold between the months of April and June, but there was no medicine as we lived far from any clinic or hospital.

One morning, as the sun began to rise, I came over a hill into a valley covered in a thick mist. Everything was still. The vegetation was covered in a thin white blanket of dew, still, new and fresh. I stopped walking, in awe of the beauty. Suddenly I felt very close to God. It was as if he was right there with me.

'Heavenly father, please let me become a priest, and a hero like Rwagasore,' I prayed out loud in Kirundi, the language we spoke at home. It was a desire I prayed often.

My family were Catholics and we went to mass each Sunday. My father had dreams of me becoming a Catholic priest. He had promised one of his children to the church, but my older siblings had all refused. Becoming a priest seemed like a good idea to me. I thought of the Italian missionary priests who came once a month to our village – they received both honour and respect. They also had a car!

I had heard all about the twenty-nine-year-old Prince Louis Rwagasore from stories my father told me. Before I was born, my father was fighting alongside Rwagasore for independence from the Belgian colonisers. But in 1961 Prince Louis was assassinated, three weeks into his role as Prime Minster after a landslide victory. He was dining with his cabinet members at the Hotel Tanganyika in Usumbura when he was killed with a single shot to the neck. Members of the Belgian-supported rival party, *Parti Démocratique Chrétien* (PDC), were blamed and put to death for the crime. Rwagasore's death was devastating for the country.

My father told me that when he heard on the radio that the prince had been killed, he lost all his courage and was fearful for his life. However, he kept fighting. A year later, in 1962, Burundi won independence from Belgium. In 1966 a coup replaced the monarchy with a one-party republic. Over the next twenty-seven years, Burundi was ruled by a series of dictators, with a horrific genocide of Hutus in 1972, two years before I was born.

Papa would tell me what a deep sadness that was for Burundi. As I was his last child, and the only one still at home, we spent a lot of time together. My father would teach me by telling me stories as we played card games together. It wasn't only the politics and history of our country he was sharing with me. He also trained me in agriculture, giving me farming projects and space to grow my own beans, bananas and sweet bananas.

Time with my dad was my favourite thing, and hearing his disappointment with the politics of our country made me long to pick up where Prince Rwagasore left off and lead my country to flourish.

When I was around twelve years old, we started hearing news on the radio of killings between Hutu and Tutsi. I didn't know the difference between the two; I understood we were all one people. Later I learnt that Belgium wanted to differentiate between tribes. They had given power to the Tutsi, who historically were cow herders, and this caused tension with the majority Hutu.

My father never spoke about this tribal friction, as he did not want me to see my Burundian brother as less than or different from me. But then one day, in school, our teacher had to fill out forms about our nationality and religion. He called out the questions in class, and when he asked me my nationality, I said, 'I'm Burundian.'

Half of the class shouted, 'He's lying!'

I looked at a close friend and asked him, 'Why do you say that I'm lying?'

'Tutsis are not Burundian,' he said.

I was very shocked. I didn't even know I was a Tutsi.

'Am I not Burundian, Papa?' I asked my dad as soon as I got home.

'Who told you that?' he asked.

'My classmates. They said Tutsi are not Burundian.'

'We are not Tutsi or Hutu, we are Burundian,' he replied firmly, but I sensed he was worried.

My family is from the royal family, who historically were rulers of the kingdoms. People say they are Tutsi because they are tall, which is a trait of the Tutsi. But because we were raised to govern and must not show partiality, the royal family does not come under one tribe. In fact, in most cases their marriages are mixed – a Tutsi father with a Hutu wife.

Every evening we continued to listen to the news on the radio at 7 p.m. (The only exception was a brief spell when our radio was stolen, but the thief could not turn the sound off, so we followed the noise and retrieved it!) We had no electricity, TV or telephone, so the radio was precious and the only way to get information. I would sit on the floor, hearing reports of killings. Now I was scared these would reach us too.

I failed sixth grade for the third time – in Burundi, you could not move forward to the next grade until you passed. My parents decided I needed to go to a better school to prepare me to join a Catholic seminary and become a priest.

Bururi, Burundi – 1993

In 1991, aged seventeen, I left home to go to boarding school in Bururi, 200 kilometres from home in southern Burundi. Two years later, in June 1993, elections were held with Melchior Ndadaye becoming the first democratically elected Hutu president.

In the July holidays I took a bus back home. There were not many buses running, so the journey, which should have taken about six hours, lasted nearly three days. When I arrived, the atmosphere in the village felt tense. 'You Tutsis should go back to where you came from,' someone shouted at me.

Now there was a Hutu president, and because my father had been involved in politics, they wanted my dad punished. I felt very uneasy and tried to get my parents to move to the town where it was safer. I found them a place, but my father kept on making excuses.

'We will be safe here in the village, everyone knows us,' he told me. He was adamant, reminding me once more that we are from the royal family, so we are neither Hutu nor Tutsi. There was nothing more I could do, so I went back to school.

On 21 October 1993 a Tutsi-dominated army faction attempted a coup. President Ndadaye was assassinated and the civil war started again, mainly in the north where my parents were. But as there were no telephone lines, I didn't know exactly what was going on. We were somewhat protected in the south.

After the coup, though, all the Hutu teachers who had been brought in to manage my school fled, worried Tutsi pupils would take revenge on them. In total, about half of the teachers and pupils left. The pupils who remained tried to keep the school going. As I had been my class representative, and later became head boy of the whole school, I was elected to be one of its leaders.

We were a co-ed school of about 2,000 learners. In November 1993 I realised we had to do something for the children who were sick – there were a few with malaria and other issues. I took charge and got our driver to take us to hospital in the school's open-backed truck. We had to wait a while for the sick to be seen by a doctor, so I stepped outside to talk to the people about what was going on in the country. While I was there, my father's cousin walked past. He was working in a school in the city.

'Dieudonne!' he greeted me with a hug, but he looked concerned, adding, 'My condolences.'

'For what?' I asked.

'Surely you know your father was killed?'

I felt as if I had been punched in the stomach.

'No, that is not true,' I said.

'It was about two weeks ago. Many people have been killed. We don't know the exact details of how it happened, and they haven't found the body. I am sorry.'

I did not cry, but I thanked him for telling me. I could not believe it was true. I had been so close to my father, I could not contemplate him being murdered.

Still not showing my grief, I took the pupils back to school. A few hours later I was told someone had sneaked into the school and, as the leader, I was asked if I wanted to kill him.

I would never kill because of an important lesson my father had taught me when I was five years old.

He had shown me an insect and said, 'Kill it, my son.' So I did.

'Now, bring it back to life,' he asked.

I tried, but obviously I could not.

'This is to show you that you must never take what you can't give back.'

It was a lesson that I took to heart. I understood I could not give life back.

So instead of killing the trespasser, I took him aside and screamed and shouted at him, terrifying him, letting out all the grief inside me.

Life continued to be unstable. I didn't know what to do. But I felt I couldn't leave school because I knew my presence was ensuring that no killing went on.

However, in early 1994 my aunt, who was a Catholic nun, came to ask if I wanted to join her in trying to go home to see what had happened. She had been able to borrow a car from a bishop connected to my school. I agreed straight away, even though I felt such a responsibility for the school.

Taking the main road, which went to Tanzania, my aunt and I arrived at a refugee camp in the early afternoon. It was there I found my mother. We both cried as we hugged each other. She had not been back to the village since my father had been killed. Part of me had been believing my father was still alive, but seeing my mother confirmed he was dead, and I was devastated.

She explained he was killed because he was a Tutsi. It was people who were professing to be Christians or

Catholics who had murdered him. That had a big impact on me, and I gave up believing in God. My father had been very faithful, going to church every Sunday, and yet he was killed by the very people we all went with to church.

My mum survived because at that time they were not killing most women – just men and pregnant women, in case they were giving birth to boys.

Others in my situation would have joined the rebel groups seeking revenge through violence. I knew even then that violence was not the answer, and that the only way to stop the horror was to somehow change the ideology of killing, but I did not know how.

I was very angry, but also knew I would be next on the list to be murdered. I had lost my faith and hope for the future. I went back to school for a few weeks until there was a ceremony to be held for my father in Bujumbura. While I was away, three students were murdered by other pupils. It was heartbreaking for me, especially as I knew they had happened because I was absent. The Minister for Education and the army went to close the school. As I heard this news while still in Bujumbura, all I could do was stay there, hoping to enrol in another school. I was homeless, and the civil war had now entered the city. Road closures, killings and fires were everywhere.

Bujumbura, Burundi – 1995

I tried to find places to stay. I had a family member in the city, but their house was full of kids and refugees from other areas; I knew I could not stay there. I also wanted to show I was a strong man and could look after myself. I realised my only option was to survive on the streets.

It was a terrifying time. I saw death almost daily – people were being shot and burned to death. Everyone was trying to flee the country. I had decided I was not going to try to leave, because I had made a commitment to be part of the change in my country; I just still didn't know how I was going to do that.

Every day I fought hopelessness. I felt rejected by family and society. But I didn't want to give up, and I also didn't want to join those who were killing. I knew trying to find a way to get to my mother was not an option – I didn't want to give her the added pressure of having to look after me as well.

Through it all I was maturing quickly, as I had to learn how to survive. I had grown up with my parents doing everything for me; now I had to fight for myself, and keep hope for the future.

I ended up living on the streets for seven months. There were many other young people like me, and I became the leader of a ragtag group of street kids. We would sleep in abandoned buildings, or any safe place we could find, and scavenge for food, sometimes getting leftover scraps from hotels.

One day I was walking along the street, wondering where I was going to get something to eat for the day, when someone called my name.

'Hey, brother, what are you doing?'

It was my friend from school, Yves Nyongera. He told me he was studying at the university. When I explained I was homeless, he invited me to stay with him. I was so grateful. At last I had some safety, and I was able to enrol at another school.

Yves was a Christian, and I used to debate with him that there was no God.

'I am sure Jesus was a good man, like Nelson Mandela, but he is not God,' I said.

Yves encouraged me to read the Bible.

I said that I was no longer interested, but at the same time I had respect for him because he was the one who helped me. So I decided, 'Okay, give me a Bible. I'm going to use it to show you that there is no God.'

He gave me a Gideon New Testament Bible and I started by reading Matthew's Gospel. The first chapters were not really interesting to me, but then I got to chapter five. In Matthew 5:43–44, Jesus says, 'You have heard that it was said, "Love your neighbour and hate your enemy." But I tell you, love your enemies and pray for those who persecute you.'

As I read it, I felt like someone was with me in the room. I was trying to prove there is no God, but the presence of God was there when I was reading. I started to cry.

'Do you want me to love those who killed my father?' I asked out loud.

The presence of God felt more intense in the room. I was overwhelmed by it.

'I choose to forgive,' I said.

Suddenly a supernatural peace fell on me, embracing me, and I wept and wept. Deep pain was coming out.

I kept on reading Matthew's Gospel and realised I could no longer say there's no God, because I felt his presence.

Yves came back to the room. 'What happened?' he asked, seeing my expression.

I didn't want to tell him I had found God, but I think he sensed it. He started to talk about love and forgiveness and then he prayed with me.

A few days later another friend invited me to a breakfast prayer meeting. The lure of breakfast was strong as I had very little food at that time. So the next morning I walked into the restaurant for the Full Gospel Businessmen's meeting. There were around thirty-five high-powered Burundians there, all from different churches around the city. It was the first time I had seen people from different denominations together.

The guest speaker, from the Democratic Republic of Congo, seemed to be speaking directly to me. He gave answers to all my questions – mainly about the actions of people who professed to be Christian but had killed my father. He explained four spiritual truths. First, God loves you and has a wonderful plan for your life. Second, man's sin separates him from God, and therefore he cannot experience God's love and plan for his life. Third, Jesus Christ is God's only provision for man's sin, enabling reconciliation with God. Finally, we must individually receive Jesus Christ as Saviour and Lord to know this salvation and peace with God. The speaker then asked who wanted to accept Jesus. I was the only one who went forward.

The group invited me to attend their meeting every Thursday. I was not ready to go to church, though, as I had been told since I was a child that Protestants worship the devil. In the end they insisted I join a church, and I initially went back to my Catholic church. But one Wednesday evening I was invited to a worship session at another church called *Eglise Vivante*. I felt the presence of God in the place and it became my church from 1996 until 2007, when I felt God direct me to lead my own church.

Bujumbura, Burundi – 1998

On Christmas Day 1998 I went to *Eglise Vivante*. When the service finished, I spoke to an older Canadian lady who had just arrived in Burundi. She asked me what I was going to do for the rest of the day.

'I'm going back to my room on the university campus,' I said, as I had no family to celebrate with.

She gave me 5,000 Burundian francs, which was approximately $5. I was so happy, as that was all the money I had. I decided to go to the shores of our beautiful Lake Tanganyika and have a Fanta on the beach to celebrate.

I walked out of church, but as I was making my way to the city centre, I saw a group of street children sitting on the ground. I knew the life they were living, as it had been mine not so long ago. I felt in my heart that I should go and talk to them.

I bought some bread and soda for them with the 5,000 francs and we sang Christmas songs together. As they were joyfully singing, I saw how happy they were.

Then I felt God speak to my heart. He said, 'You are no longer an orphan. I want you to help these children, because I am going to use them to change the nation.'

So, at the start of 1999, I spent five days in prayer asking God what he wanted me to do. I sensed him say, 'I want you to reach young people using New Generation as a tool.'

New Generation was a club I had started while at boarding school. Now God gave me the vision for New Generation to be a movement of young people to bring revival, starting with orphans.

My next step was to start gathering friends from church. We would meet every Thursday to pray and feed the children in a building that had been abandoned by the government. By 2000 we were feeding about 200 street kids every day. We had no funding, but God provided day by day.

One time we had no food left and no money. I told the children our need and we all prayed together, asking God to provide.

Suddenly my friend, Simon Guillebaud, arrived with trays of delicious leftover food from a function he had been to in a hotel. The street children celebrated with shouts of joy. They feasted that evening, and we praised God who again showed us his goodness and power to provide what we needed.

It was in those early days that I met my wife, Mariam. She grew up in a Muslim family, but had become a Christian and was volunteering with us. We fell in love, but it was hard to convince her parents that she should marry me, a man without a home or a proper job.

Only God could help me, and he did.

I was connected to a Swedish businessman, who asked me to show him around Bujumbura. He had business in Burundi, and would be coming and going, so asked me to find a house for him to rent for two weeks.

I found a house, and then he asked me to show him the Catholic orphanage, as he wanted to support them.

'What do you do?' he next asked.

I told him I just take care of street kids.

He seemed interested. 'Can you show me where you do that?'

I said, 'Of course,' and he came along to where we were feeding about 200 street kids. They were all sitting on the floor waiting for the food.

'Who funds you?' he asked, incredulous.

'What do you mean?' I replied, not understanding the question.

'Who gives you money to feed all these children?'

I told him our situation – that no one gave us money, but we got some leftover food from hotels and God provided in different ways.

He was shocked, and decided he would support us instead of the Catholic orphanage, as they already had funding through the church.

'If you can find me a proper house to rent here, fully furnished, you can live there and take care of it,' he said.

After talking to some people, we found a place, fully equipped. The rent was $500 a month, but I was living there for free.

During that time the police had found the street kids sleeping in the abandoned building and put them in prison. There was lots of shooting in the city and it was very dangerous. I explained the situation to the Swedish man, and he agreed to let me take thirty of the youngest street kids to stay with me in the house. Initially the landlord said no to this plan, but he then agreed when the rent was increased slightly.

I invited Mariam's family over and they were amazed!

Not long after the businessman came back for two months and gave me a laptop, the first I had owned. He wanted to rent a car, but as someone from church was selling theirs, he instead bought that so I could use it when he was away.

I had a car and a home! Now I just needed a job.

After praying, I went along to the French cultural centre. They had new computers that I started to help the young people understand how to use. When someone saw me teaching, they asked me to be a teacher at the French school. I met the principal, who said they had just received twenty-four computers and needed someone to teach computer skills. I had no formal training, but I told myself that the Holy Spirit knows everything so I know everything, and I accepted the job.

I now had a house, a car *and* a job! I was ecstatic when Mariam's family finally agreed for us to be married. Our wedding was in 2001.

Muyinga, Burundi – 2003

Ten years after my father was killed, the civil war was ongoing in Bujumbura and ethnic groups were very divided. The programme of peace and reconciliation with the New Generation youth movement continued. But I realised that although I had forgiven the man who had taken my father's life many years before – he was a leader in our church – I didn't know how I would react when I saw him face to face.

I heard the area where I grew up was becoming calmer, so I managed to organise a team of young people from New Generation to go there, and we rented a bus. It was my first time back in ten years. The purpose of our trip was to lead an evangelism crusade.

After we had arrived and started to set up, I suddenly saw the man who had killed my father. He was there with other people who had come to see us. I went straight up to him, and knew at that moment I had been really changed by the word of God, because there was no anger in me – I just wanted to go and greet him and hug him. When I got close to him, he did not recognise me because I was now a man.

I greeted him, saying, 'I am Dieudonne Nahimana.' His face fell and I could tell he wanted to run away, but I stopped him. 'Don't worry,' I said. 'I forgave you a long time ago, because God forgave my sins.' He calmed down, and I even took a picture with him. In my heart all I wanted was to see him saved and come to Jesus, because I saw he was really suffering.

I preached in our crusade and many came forward to give their life to Jesus. But this man didn't take the first step that day.

I decided to come back in a few weeks, again with some New Generation students, to bring clothes for the kids – there were so many naked children, mainly from the poorer Batwa tribe, who didn't have any clothing. This man came from the back of the crowd and asked, 'Can you please give some clothes to my daughter?' Turning around and seeing him, I suddenly felt in my heart I needed to give clothes to his children, even if he wasn't on the list. As I handed him some clothes, a heavy weight left my shoulders. I realised forgiveness is not just words; it is also action. You need to do good to those you forgive. That was a powerful revelation for me.

When I went back home and told my wife what had happened, and how it gave me such joy, we discussed that even with the little we had, we wanted to try and support his children. So I returned again and told his wife that we would pay for his kids' school fees and uniform. She was overwhelmed. When her husband passed away in 2017, we promised to continue supporting his kids. Two of them have already graduated from school and recently one of his kids arrived in Bujumbura bringing some of their crops to thank us for supporting him in his studies. I was really touched.

We stay very close to the kids of the man who killed my father. They know what happened, but they also understand the forgiveness of God that sets us free.

Rio de Janeiro, Brazil – 2014

I had the opportunity to go with eleven Burundian street kids to compete in the Street Child World Cup in Brazil. I could not believe how far we had come! We travelled from Bujumbura to Kigali to Nairobi to Dubai, where we boarded a plane headed for Rio de Janeiro.

I had heard about the Street Child World Cup after being invited to the UK in 2013 to be part of the Street Action UK Conference. It was there I met the founders of the Street Child World Cup, and they encouraged me to apply. I was teaching myself English at this point, from TV and by listening to English-speaking preachers. It was my fourth language after Kirundi, Swahili and French.

Our flights were paid for by a sponsor in the UK, but we had no sports kit or boots. While we had no expectation to win, we were all very excited!

I was not able to take a professional football coach with us, but when the team started to play, we were amazed to see that we were winning! We got into the semi-final with Pakistan, which was nerve-racking as they were the strongest team.

After the first half, it was 3-0 to Pakistan. Our team were very discouraged. At half-time I went onto the field to speak to them.

'What happened?' I asked.

They started to blame each other for not passing the ball, or not scoring when they should have. They were all putting the fault on one another.

'Boys, what has New Generation taught you?'

There was a silence, and shuffling of feet.

'Forgiveness,' said one of the boys.

'What do you need to do now?' I asked.

The first boy, Innocent, said to his teammates, 'I am sorry, it was my fault.'

Another, then another, all started apologising. We then held hands on the middle of the pitch, with the crowds watching us, and started to pray.

'Everything is possible to them who believe,' I told the team, as they ran off to take their positions.

In the second half our Burundian team fought back to win the match 4-3! Everyone was amazed. It was a powerful message for the children that God is able to help those who put his word into practice.

Through the experience in Brazil God was bringing visibility to New Generation and our work, just when we needed it.

Bujumbura, Burundi – 2024

Since the beginning of New Generation, it had been my vision to raise up the next generation of leaders from among the street kids. We had trained more than 10,000 young people through New Generation, teaching them about servant leadership, honour and integrity. In 2000 it was my dream to have a presidential candidate by 2020.

In 2018, after three terms in office, President Pierre Nkurunziza decided to step down. I felt in my heart it was the right time to finally put forward a candidate to run for the presidential elections. I called back some of my best trainees, who were now people of influence and responsibility in different institutions. We did a refresher leadership course with them, with the purpose of encouraging them to stand and run as a presidential candidate. When we finished the course, they all said, 'You have been telling us to stand, but we think you have everything required to stand yourself and be an example to us.'

I took three months to pray about what they were suggesting. I visited my key spiritual leaders, asking them what they thought, and it became very clear that I should put myself forward.

I decided not to run as part of a political party, but as an independent candidate. It was the first time an independent candidate had stood for election in Burundi. However, in the end, Évariste Ndayishimiye of the ruling CNDD–FDD party was elected president. Our next presidential elections are expected in May 2027, and in 2025 there will be elections for members of parliament. I may consider running as an MP, and then as a presidential candidate in 2027.

For now, in 2024, my desire is to continue to raise up young leaders in the country, along with my wife and our four children, Nathan, Tracy, Zoë and Grace.

All those years ago, while running to school in the bush, I asked God to be a Catholic priest and a hero of independence. I am now a pastor to a church filled with the forgotten ones of this world. I have entered politics, not to be a hero, but to see the blessing and flourishing of our nation, and to see an end to ethnic violence. I pray that there will be no more death, and that the Burundians would live in harmony with one another.

7

MARCIA SUZUKI

BRAZIL

Rio de Janeiro – 1970

I was born in Rio de Janeiro, Brazil. My parents were not religious, but I used to watch my neighbours go to church each Sunday and longed to go too – they looked so happy. When I was seven, I suggested to my younger sister, Margaret, that we ask the neighbours to take us with them. The plan worked; they were surprised but delighted, and agreed straight away. To get my parents' approval, I lied, saying they had invited us.

The following Sunday we arrived at the Methodist church and followed the other children to Sunday school. A woman began telling us a story about what Jesus had done on the cross. My heart was captured and I hung on her every word. At the end of the talk, the teacher asked if anyone wanted to accept Jesus into their lives. I had no doubts. So that Sunday morning, Jesus became my Lord. Excitedly I went home to tell my parents. My mother seemed pleased, but my dad was uninterested.

They let me continue to attend church. Once, when I was ten, a missionary came to preach. It was the first time I heard about missionaries and my heart soared with excitement. 'I want to be a missionary,' I told my parents as soon as I got home. I think they hoped it was a passing phase.

The next year there was a big Bible quiz at church. It was mostly for the adults, but I was allowed to join in. To my amazement, even as the youngest in the competition, I won. The prize was a weeklong trip to a Christian camp called *Palavra da Vida*. The camp had a big impact on the rest of my life. Many missionaries spoke and their stories inspired me. One evening, after a talk, people were asked if they wanted to commit their lives to serving the Lord. A huge fire was built and every person who felt called took a stick or branch to add to it. I picked up my stick and walked to the fire, telling God I would go anywhere for him. As I threw my stick into the fire and watched the flames get brighter and stronger, I realised that I could make a difference, even though I was young.

I came home and excitedly told my parents what I had done.

'That is ridiculous,' my father shouted. 'What kind of life is being a missionary? It's for people who don't work, not for *my* daughter.'

He was very upset, and I was devastated. I couldn't convince him to trust my decision, and it was so hard to go against his wishes. Our relationship was deeply affected, and I missed my father's closeness. However I couldn't give up what I felt was a call to the mission field.

When I was fourteen, I decided it was time I got out there. I wrote to every missionary organisation I had ever heard of, asking them if I could join. To my disappointment they all wrote back saying I was too young; I should finish my studies and then contact them again. Then I heard of the organisation Youth With A Mission (YWAM). Surely a mission with a name like that would take young people? But they too said I was too young. I was very frustrated until they contacted me a little while later saying I could join them for a month-long outreach over the winter holidays. Even though sixteen was the age required for the trip (by this time I was fifteen), they decided to give me a chance because I had been so insistent and written them so many letters begging to come.

With a group of thirty other young people, I went to a city in the Minas Gerais region of Brazil. It wasn't easy or comfortable. The girls slept in the damp cold basement of the church. Every morning we woke up to find the wooden walls wet with humidity. We didn't have much money for food either. But I didn't mind at all. I loved the whole experience, and was in my element telling people about Jesus, loving them and showing them how much God loved them.

At seventeen, when I finished school, I applied to take part in their Discipleship Training School (DTS) at the only YWAM base in Brazil at the time – in Contagem, near Belo Horizonte. Again I was officially too young for the course, but they made an exception and I was allowed to attend. While I was there, God spoke to me about my future. Hearing for the first time about the Amazon Indians in the north of Brazil, something about them touched me and I felt God say he wanted me to go to those people. I also felt my time with the Indians would be my equivalent of a university education. When I broke the news to my parents, my dad was dead set against it. He didn't talk to me for almost a year after I made the decision.

Maxakali tribe, Minas Gerais – 1982

While at DTS, I came across Wycliffe Bible Translators, who work with different tribes. In the summer of 1982 I began a three-month training course with Wycliffe in Brasilia. It was the first time I had studied linguistics and I loved it, so much so that I advanced to the top of the class. In the last week a Canadian couple invited me to come with them to the Maxakali, a tribe in the state of Minas Gerais. The couple had been missionaries with Wycliffe for many years, and were now starting a literacy programme among the Maxakali.

I arrived in May and lived in a house in the Maxakali village with a group of students from Minas Gerais University. They were part of a programme run by the anthropology department, trying to help the Maxakali overcome their alcohol problems. My job was to teach the Indians to read and write in their own language.

It was a heartbreaking time. The Maxakali were often drunk and would fight and try to kill each other.

Countless times I had to get in the middle of a fight to split up the sparing Indians. One lady I worked with was murdered by her husband when he was drunk. On the weekends the other students and I had to bar ourselves into our house as ten to twenty drunk Indians would come in the middle of the night to try to get in and rape us.

I was the only Christian in the house, so I would pray continually, sometimes out loud. It was a baptism of fire into the Indian culture, but God supernaturally increased my heart and love for the people.

I had no financial support the whole time I was with the tribe. My mother sent money, but a problem with the bank meant it never arrived. Each day I prayed in faith, asking God to provide. I knew he could, so didn't understand why no provision came.

'Where is your God now?' laughed the other students. I cried every day at my situation, but held on to my faith. I was allowed to receive meals with the other students, as I promised to pay them back, but had no idea how the money would come. It was the hardest test to learn to obey God even when he did not give me what I wanted when I wanted.

One evening, as I was on my knees crying out to God, I felt he spoke to my heart: 'After this time you will never have problems with money again.'

On the last day a Christian anthropologist from the university came to visit. When she heard from the other students that I had no money, she paid all my expenses in full. My heart melted, and I praised God who was fulfilling his promises to me.

When I said goodbye to the tribe after three months, I cried. I didn't want to leave, but felt God was telling me to go to the Amazon.

Sateré-Mawé tribe, Amazon – 1982

I heard about the Sateré-Mawé tribe from Gerson Ribeiro, one of my YWAM leaders. Their chief, a man called Kadete, realised that his people were destroying themselves through alcohol and fighting each other. Though he knew he was supposed to lead, he didn't know what to do. When he finally had enough, unable to stand by and watch the tribe self-destruct, he decided to abandon them and move to the city. He took a canoe and travelled to Manaus. There he got drunk, was beaten up and became destitute. After several years in Manaus, he was walking in a poor neighbourhood when he was attracted by the sound of singing coming from a building nearby. Going to take a closer look, he walked into a small church service.

He understood the gospel message that was being preached. 'This is Tupana that you are talking about!' he explained. Tupana was the Sateré-Mawé name for God. But this was the first time Kadete had heard of Tupana as a loving God. Kadete asked the pastor to come with him to tell the tribe about Jesus, but the pastor could not. Kadete then persuaded someone to write to the churches in Brazil. The letter, written in Kadete's name, stated that he was the chief of his Sateré-Mawé village in the Amazon. It asked for someone to come and live with the tribe and teach them about Jesus.

While the letter was sent from church to church, Kadete excitedly went back to his people to prepare a place for the missionaries. He built a new hut for them, and planted manioc and sugar cane for them to eat. But the weeks went by, then months, then years. No one came.

By this time a pastor had made copies of the letter, one of which reached a missionary conference in the south of Brazil. Gerson Ribeiro was there. When he heard the letter read, he felt God speak to him. As he got up to preach, he said that he knew a missionary who would go to the Sateré-Mawé. He was thinking of me.

A week or so later Gerson came back to the YWAM base in Belem. When I heard about Kadete, I knew this was the tribe God had prepared me for. I would be their missionary.

In September 1982 I journeyed with Gerson and two other YWAMers into the Amazon to meet the tribe. We travelled for the first five days in a very comfortable tourist boat. We then transferred to a smaller boat used by gold miners. Eventually reaching the Amazonian city of Maués, we got into a large canoe with a roof and outboard motor for the forty-eight-hour trip to the Sateré-Mawé. When we arrived in Atuka, the villagers were very warm and welcoming. Kadete was so touched we had come that he couldn't speak.

A couple of years later, one of the Sateré-Mawé women, Isabel, told me her story. Before we arrived she had been having problems with her family. Her sons were always drunk and her husband had sold their daughter to outsiders to pay off a debt. Isabel was so depressed she was thinking of suicide. One night she had a dream in which she saw four angels laughing, dancing and praising God under a rainbow. When she woke up, a spark of hope stayed with her that maybe God would send someone to help.

The next day she was washing her clothes by the water's edge when she heard the putt-putt of a boat engine. She looked up and saw the four of us dancing and shouting on the roof, with a rainbow over our heads in the sky. Immediately she remembered her dream and ran to the villagers. It was because of Isabel that our reception had been so warm.

I worked with the Sateré-Mawé for three years, until in 1985 I felt my time with the tribe was coming to an end. Gerson said he thought my gift was language study and therefore I should start with a new tribe to analyse their language. He told me about the Suruwahá tribe, and I felt a growing love for them as I prayed.

Suruwahá tribe – 1990

Before I went to the Suruwahá, I took a month-long linguistics course held by the Federal University of Pará. A fellow Brazilian YWAMer, Edson Suzuki (called 'Suzuki' by his friends), was on the course with me. We had known each other for a few years, often taking boats together with other team members when travelling in and out of the Amazon. We had an instant connection, and I was always happy around him. Though we spent lots of time together, I had no inclination that he liked me romantically. At the end of the course nothing happened, although Gerson would tease me saying, 'He loves you!'

I went home to Rio for five months to try and raise funds to go to Melbourne, Australia to study at the South Pacific Summer Institute of Linguistics. It was very hard raising the money needed, even though every weekend I would speak at churches about what I was doing.

'Lord, you promised to provide,' I prayed, remembering the lesson I had learnt with the Maxakali Indians. God does not forget his promises.

I went to talk to the bishop of my region. He was very touched, and decided to send a message to all the Methodist churches in Rio telling them to give next Sunday's offering to me. I was overwhelmed; it was exactly enough for me to travel to Australia and live there for a year.

The first letter I received in Australia was from Suzuki. I nearly fainted when I read it. He poured out his heart to me, saying he loved me, he missed me and he wanted to be with me for the rest of his life! I was overwhelmed with joy! I loved him too.

At the end of 1989, after the course finished, I flew back to Brazil. Suzuki invited me to São Paulo to meet his family and asked my father for my hand in marriage. We married in July 1990.

After our two-week honeymoon, we gathered our belongings to move to the new YWAM base in Porto Velho. We planned to build a house near the Suruwahá, but there were many difficulties. The place was only accessible by boat and it would take a month and a half to travel to the spot where we could build a house. In addition, it could only be reached for a short window of time during the year, otherwise the Coxodoá river was too low for navigation. We would have to work quickly before the water level dropped so we weren't stranded in the middle of the jungle for a year without food. The jungle is a very dangerous and inhospitable place for everyone, even for the Indians. You need survival skills just to journey out into the jungle to find food, and then there is the danger of jaguars, snakes and malaria.

Having built the YWAM base by June 1991, we finally went to visit the Suruwahá. Suzuki had lived with them for many years before we married. As I followed him along the jungle trail to find the tribe, it was tiring work: the jungle was steaming hot, but we were covered in clothing to protect our skin from insect bites.

When we were nearly there, we took a short breather. Suddenly I heard a noise along the trail and in an instant we were surrounded by the Suruwahá. My first impression was terror – all I saw were men who were naked, painted red and with bows and arrows directed straight at me. Suzuki did not seem worried at all. 'It's my wife!' he said, presenting me to them. (Suzuki had told the tribe he would come back with a wife before I had said yes!) They were so intrigued that they wanted to take my clothes off to inspect me more. As quickly as they tried to peel away my clothing, I put it back on!

The villagers danced all night in celebration of our arrival – in the centre of the big round longhouse, arms linked over their shoulders. I was exhausted. Eventually Suzuki was able to locate my hammock and set it up for me.

The people had previously decided Suzuki must be some kind of shaman because he would go into the jungle and sing loudly to Jesus. Singing is something very special to the tribe: 'He is not a hunter, he is not strong, but he must have contact with spirits because he sings. He is *inuwa.*'

From then on, if a young man went out hunting and took too long to return, his mother would often come to Suzuki to pray that her son would be safe.

'Close your eyes and see where my son is. Is he safe?' she would ask.

We believe that God gave us that opportunity as an open door to explain who he is and reveal his power.

'Suzuki, the things you talk about – when did they happen?' the Suruwahá men would ask.

Suzuki explained that Jesus died a long, long time ago.

'But Suzuki,' they would reply, laughing, 'we could show you a tree in the jungle today, and tomorrow you would forget it. How can you remember these stories from so long ago?'

We realised that the Suruwahá would never believe by being convinced in their minds – Suzuki had tried many times to tell them about God. They had to experience the power and presence of the living God.

One day the daughter of the shaman, Asia, committed suicide. (It was a common way to die in the tribe, if anything had upset or hurt a person.) Asia was devastated and decided to commit suicide himself. But as he ran through the jungle to find the poison root, Jesus appeared in front of him!

Jesus told Asia not to follow his daughter but to go back to the tribe and live. Asia ran back and immediately came to find us.

'I saw Jesus! He told me not to commit suicide,' he exclaimed.

Suzuki and I looked at each other in surprise.

'What did he look like?' Suzuki asked.

'Like us – he was naked and painted red, but he was big and strong!'

'How did you know it was Jesus?' I asked.

'I know many spirits, but I knew this was Jesus because he was different,' Asia said. 'His eyes were shining like fire. And when he spoke, his voice was so powerful, but it was also gentle.'

We were excited, but also not a hundred per cent certain of what had happened. I felt if he really had seen Jesus, Asia would change. You cannot meet with the living God and stay the same. And over the next few days and weeks, Asia transformed. His heart reached out to the needy, widows and orphans in the tribe.

Shamans often went into the jungle at night and sang to get possessed by spirits. Then they came back and passed on the song to their tribe. One day Suzuki and I returned after two weeks away to hear that Asia had gone into the jungle to sing. The whole tribe had been touched by the most beautiful song and were still speaking about it.

Suzuki and I felt deflated. We were sure Asia knew Jesus, but it sounded like he was still being possessed by spirits.

Later, when we heard the descriptions of his song, we were taken aback. He was singing about an angel walking along a trail in heaven, beside a plantation of cashew fruit. The cashew fruit represents the heart: it has the same shape and colour. The red of the fruit was standing out brightly against the green of the leaves. As the angel walked away, he saw a log on the trail. On it were cashew nuts, but without the fruit to which they were normally attached.

'Who ate the fruit?' the angel asked.

'It must have been Jesus,' Asia said. 'Jesus ate the fruit and made my heart sweet.'

The song was so symbolic, explaining perfectly how Jesus is our atonement, taking away our sin. It also described the transformation of our hearts when we welcome Jesus in. The song was infinitely better than how Suzuki or I could have explained the gospel.

From Porto Velho to São Paulo – 2000

After thirteen years with the Suruwahá, we left the jungle, but we left as parents. Suzuki and I had assumed we would not have children because of the life we led. But in May 2000, when we were staying at the Porto Velho

YWAM base, an American pastor, Mike Shea, visited. One morning over breakfast, he told us he felt God was saying we would have a child at the end of the year.

'That's impossible!' I laughed.

I was perfectly content without children and we were not trying for a family. Even if I became pregnant that day, a baby born nine months later would not be in the same calendar year.

Mike was very humble: 'Okay, maybe I got it wrong. I'll go back and pray about it some more.'

A few days later he was even more adamant. 'I really think God is saying you will have a child by the end of the year who will be a blessing to the Suruwahá,' he said.

Suzuki and I thanked him, and I promptly forgot all about it.

There was a couple in the tribe, Dihiji and Bujini, who had three sons. But when their fourth son, Niawi, was a year old, people started to notice that there was something wrong with him; he wasn't developing normally.

'He has no soul, you have to kill him,' the villagers said to his parents. This is a common Suruwahá belief about any child with a deformity. If the child is not buried alive, poisoned or abandoned in the jungle, they believe it will bring bad luck on the tribe.

But the couple loved their little boy and didn't want to kill him. They tried to hide him and keep out of people's way. Under so much pressure, they became withdrawn and depressed.

From then on, if anything went wrong with the tribe, it was blamed on Niawi. When his mother became pregnant again, she was terrified that the curse would repeat itself. She gave birth in July 1995 to a girl, Hakani, but after two years her parents realised she had the same problems as her brother Niawi.

They tried many times to poison themselves as they could not deal with the pressure. At one point Suzuki and I had to go to Porto Velho to teach at a cross-cultural training school. While we were there, Dihiji and Bujini both succeeded in committing suicide. The tribe then took Niawi and Hakani to bury them alive.

Niawi died, but Hakani was saved by her older brother, Bibi. We heard about the deaths upon our return. Hakani was kept at the edge of the hut, or in the bushes nearby; no one cared for her. We tried to feed Hakani, but every time the Indians took the food and told us that it was theirs, not ours. Many times we asked the Indian leaders if we could bring Hakani out of the tribe for medical care, but they wouldn't let us. The government's position of non-interference meant that if we antagonised the Indians by removing Hakani against their will, we would be jailed and accused of kidnapping. As foreigners, we were also dependent on the Suruwahá for our survival and to remain in the tribe. They had adopted us and were sharing generously.

This situation was Hakani's life for three years. She was treated like a dog and beaten every day by the children. It was Bibi who kept her going. He would forage in the jungle by day and sneak food to her at night.

Sometime after her fifth birthday, in 2000, I was sure she would die. She was tiny, her skin was black and infected, and she was emaciated with a large extended stomach. One day the villagers started to say she was dead. I was so sad to see her lying lifeless on the ground, but although her body was motionless, her eyes looked up at me. She was alive.

Suzuki and I took her to the river to wash away all the dirt and filth. She was like a living corpse. We decided to pray all night for her life. It was unlikely she would survive the night, but we would try.

We went into the middle of the hut and cried out to God. The Suruwahá told us we were crazy to care for her. As dawn was beginning to break, we realised we now needed to sleep. I went over to check on her one more time, and the whole hammock we had placed her in was covered in faeces. It was disgusting – full of feathers, bones and sticks; whatever she had eaten.

After Suzuki took her to the stream to wash her, I saw that her belly had shrunk; she seemed to have more life in her. Over the next couple of days she improved quickly, but we realised her only hope of living was to get her out of the jungle to a doctor.

She was diagnosed with hypothyroidism, which, because it had been left untreated, had caused cretinism – severely stunted physical and mental growth. At five and a half years old she was the size of a toddler.

We spent the last nine months of 2001 in São Paulo while Hakani received treatment. I knew then that she was the child the pastor had said we would have. We were told she would never walk or talk, but after being loved and cared for she started walking and talking. When the doctor saw her again, tears fell down his cheeks as he said her improvement was 'impossible'.

A year later we took her back to the Suruwahá to visit. They were amazed to see her. For the first time they realised they didn't have to kill such babies.

Maués to Brasilia – 2005

We were in the Maués YWAM base when the Porto Velho YWAM base called us out of the blue because two Suruwahá families with sick children had turned up. One of these was Muwaji, a twenty-eight-year-old widow, with her nine-year-old son and a little girl, Iganani, who was sick with suspected cerebral palsy.

In previous years Muwaji and I had often talked of ways to save babies whom we knew were going to be killed. She had helped several children in the past. Now Muwaji was in the same predicament. The thought of burying Iganani was unbearable.

We were able to take the two families to São Paulo for medical help, but then started facing problems – an anthropologist wrote to the federal prosecutor in Manaus, accusing us of kidnapping the Indians.

This began a huge legal battle to be able to support the Indians. We moved to Brasilia and, from July 2006 to January 2007, lived together with the Indian families in a house. We were working with Christian lawyers and a parliamentary assessor, Dr Damares Alves, to pass Muwaji's Bill to stop infanticide in the tribes. With many miracles the bill was passed! We could now help Indian parents who did not want to kill their babies. Muwaji's Law (officially called Law Project 1057) was eventually approved at the Congressional Committee of Human Rights and Minorities in June 2011.

Since 2006, Suzuki and I also had been working on Uniskript, which is a scientific methodology that can be applied to any language to generate alphabets. It enables people to learn to read and write within days or even hours.

Hawaii and Arizona – 2011

In December 2010 we had moved with sixty Indians from different tribes to a farm called House of the Nations. It was just outside Brasilia, paid for by the generous donation of an English YWAMer. However, in 2011 we got a tip off that our lives were in danger. We had ruffled a few feathers with the passing of Muwaji's Law and were not popular among secular anthropologists.

We had to take the threat seriously, so – with little time to plan – Suzuki, Hakani and I flew to the YWAM base in Kona, Hawaii. We have not been back home to Brazil since, which is heartbreaking for us.

We spent the first four years in Hawaii mainly developing Uniskript alphabets for different languages and training people. While we couldn't leave the USA, the people we trained took Uniskript to places like Papua New Guinea as well as African and South American countries. Then we were invited to Arizona to work with the Navajo tribe. We spent nearly four years there and developed Uniskript Navajo, which the main school in the reservation uses as a tool for reading. When covid came, I was leading a Master's degree in linguistics for Bible translation in YWAM – we have trained around seventy YWAMers as Bible translators and facilitators.

Los Angeles – 2021

Our latest move was to Los Angeles in 2021, serving at the YWAM base and helping lead its global movement of oral Bible translation. In September 2024 we started a partnership with *The Jesus Film*, so now we will also be helping YWAMers to translate the film script into languages without a Bible. Our focus is education, training and multiplying.

I believe Uniskript is the perfect link between orality and literacy because it reflects the way we talk. For those who adopt Uniskript, it feels their own and helps heal the wounds of oppressive educational systems. Once people receive an oral Bible, they usually express desire to have a written one as well.

We are also seeing spiritual fruit. Suzuki is currently working with Muslim young men who wanted to preserve their three languages in South Sudan. We invited them to translate orally the books of Ruth and Jonah into their mother tongue. In the process, they gave their lives to Jesus.

Hebrews 4:12 says that the word of God is, 'living and active. Sharper than any double-edged sword, it penetrates even to dividing soul and spirit, joints and marrow; it judges the thoughts and attitudes of the heart.' There are 7,394 languages spoken in the world. According to a Wycliffe report, though, one in five people are still waiting for the Bible in their language. As God has made Suzuki and I gifted with linguistics, we are dedicating our lives to the Bible being translated into every language for every person.

CONCLUSION

BY SIMON GUILLEBAUD

What a powerful, beautiful and stirring collection of stories from a range of passionate Jesus-followers in different parts of the world! I hope you feel encouraged. We serve an amazing God!

Each of these friends of mine would say they were just ordinary people who said 'yes' to God's call and were able to do extraordinary things because God – not them – is extraordinary. They remind me of Keith Johnstone's line: 'There are people who prefer to say "yes" and there are people who prefer to say "no". Those who say "yes" are rewarded by the adventures they have. Those who say "no" are rewarded by the safety they attain.' The purpose of this book is to stir your faith; dare to dream and seek God's will as to what your life might look like.

All of us are called by God. For some that'll mean crossing oceans and jungles; for others it'll mean crossing the street or the office floor. Whatever your circumstances, have the courage to pray the prayer that took me to Burundi: 'Here I am, Lord! I'll do anything for you; I'll go anywhere for you!'

I often preach on the call of Abraham in Genesis 12, drawing out four principles that apply to all of us – wherever we are and in whatever stage of life we find ourselves. If you want the adventure of living rather than the safety of existing, you need to COME:

Claim God's promises
Obey God's commands
Maintain faith in God's leading
Embrace risks for God's glory

First, we see that Abraham claimed the wildly improbable seven-fold promise of Genesis 12:2–3:

I will make you into a great nation,
    and I will bless you;
I will make your name great,
    and you will be a blessing.
I will bless those who bless you,
    and whoever curses you I will curse;
and all peoples on earth
    will be blessed through you.

How could that possibly happen when Abraham and barren Sarah were old and wrinkly? But he trusted that promise. In Genesis 15:5–6, we read that God:

…took him outside and said, 'Look up at the sky and count the stars – if indeed you can count them.' Then he said to him, 'So shall your offspring be.'

Abram believed the LORD, and he credited it to him as righteousness.

However, Abraham couldn't just sit on the promise; he needed to obey God's command. Genesis 12:4 simply says, 'So Abram went, as the LORD had told him.' It was a big deal to pack up and leave Haran with all his extended household and animals. But he obeyed.

And when you claim God's promises and obey God's command, the next principle to grasp is that you'll have to maintain faith in God's leading through the troughs, not just on the peaks. Abraham's journey took difficult detours such as having to rescue his nephew Lot in chapter 14. Abraham actually lied about the identity of his wife Sarah – not once, but twice (in Genesis 12 and 20). This perversely encourages me – because he messed up repeatedly, just like we do. And then he faced the supreme challenge of laying down Isaac as a sacrificial offering in Genesis 22. Despite these ups and downs, Abraham maintained faith in God's leading, and the rest is history.

Critically, and finally, Abraham embraced risks for God's glory. It was a big step into the unknown when he left Haran, where he had 'settled' (11:31). The promise from 12:1 was: 'Go from your country, your people and your father's household to the land *I will show you*' (my italics). God didn't show him up front where he was to go; rather God would reveal the next step as Abraham not only claimed God's promise, obeyed God's command and maintained faith in God's leading, but also embraced unknown risks for God's glory.

All the beautiful people you've just read about likewise chose to COME, and you can too. Maybe God is calling you to stay where you are and be faithful in serving him in your current context. If so, keep going! But maybe he's calling you to step out in faith, knowing that as you come to him, he will go with you.

The key thing is to surrender our right to live our lives for ourselves and to come to Jesus in total trust. I love what Oswald Chambers wrote in *My Utmost for His Highest*:

> If you abandon everything to Jesus, and come when He says, 'Come!', then He will continue to say, 'Come,' through you. You will go out into the world reproducing the echo of Christ's 'Come.' That is the result in every soul who has abandoned all and come to Jesus.

Why not close this book with A.W. Tozer's prayer of commitment:

> I come to you today, O Lord,
> To give up my rights,
> To lay down my life,
> To offer my future,
> To give my devotion, my skills, my energies.
> I shall not waste time

Deploring my weaknesses

Nor my unfittedness for the work.

I acknowledge your choice with my life

To make your Christ attractive and intelligible

To those around me.

I come to you for spiritual preparation.

Put your hand upon me,

Anoint me with the oil of the One with Good News.

Save me from compromise,

Heal my soul from small ambitions,

Deliver me from the itch to always be right,

Save me from wasting time.

I accept hard work, I ask for no easy place,

Help me not to judge others who walk

a smoother path.

Show me those things that diminish spiritual

power in a soul.

I now consecrate my days to you,

Make your will more precious than

anybody or anything.

Fill me with your power

And when at the end of life's journey I see

you face to face

May I hear those undeserved words

'Well done you good and faithful servant'.

I ask this not for myself

But for the glory of the name of your Son.

Enough said! God bless you!

More books from 10Publishing

Resources that point to Jesus